Mind and politics

Mind and politics

*An approach to the meaning of liberal
and socialist individualism*

by Ellen Meiksins Wood

University of California Press
Berkeley, Los Angeles, London: 1972

213545

University of California Press
Berkeley and Los Angeles, California
University of California Press, Ltd.
London, England
Copyright © 1972 by The Regents of the University of California
ISBN: 0–520–02029–4
Library of Congress Catalog Card Number: 74–153556
Designed by Theo Jung
Printed in the United States of America

To my mother, Mischa,
and Neal

Acknowledgments

I have tried my thoughts out on many people, notably my husband, Neal, who as always has been very patient and very helpful, and my students, to whom I must render thanks and, no doubt, apologies. My particular gratitude goes to Professor Richard Ashcraft of the Department of Political Science, University of California, Los Angeles, whose advice has been invaluable and many of whose insights, particularly in relation to John Locke, I have quite shamelessly appropriated. Finally, I cannot omit giving thanks to the typing pool at York University, Toronto, and to Mrs. Ruth Griffin, of Glendon College, who performed miracles in helping me to meet various and sundry deadlines.

Contents

Man is in the most literal sense of the word a *zoon politikon,* not only a social animal, but an animal which can develop into an individual only in society.

KARL MARX
A Contribution to the Critique of Political Economy

An artificially induced uniformity of thought and sentiment is a symptom of an inner void . . . The "joining" habit of the average American, and his excessive sociability, may well have an explanation like that of conformity. . . . We should not be so averse to solitude if we had, when we were alone, the companionship of communal thought built into our mental habits. In the absence of this communion, there is the need for reinforcement by external contact. Our sociability is largely an effort to find substitutes for that normal consciousness of connection and union that proceeds from being a sustained and sustaining member of a social whole.

The habit of opposing the corporate and collective to the individual tends to the persistent continuation of the confusion and uncertainty. It distracts attention from the crucial issue: How shall the individual refind himself in an unprecedentedly new social situation, and what qualities will the new individualism exhibit?

I am not anxious to depict the form which this emergent individualism will assume. Indeed I do not see how it can be described until more progress has been made in its production. But such progress will not be initiated until we cease opposing the socially corporate to the individual. . . . The greatest obstacle to that vision is, I repeat, the perpetuation of the older individualism now reduced, as I have said, to . . . private pecuniary gain.

JOHN DEWEY
Individualism Old and New

Introduction

Man's speculations about the world began, it is often said, with an interpretation of nature in terms of society, and his earliest attempts to comprehend the world philosophically may have been based on principles derived from social and political order. There have also been suggestions that one sign of a culture's intellectual maturity is its conceptual separation of the natural and social realms; and yet, it is tempting to see, even in the most refined philosophical systems, traces of their political parentage. Certainly, it can be maintained that Western philosophy was born in the political experience of ancient Greece; and the three philosophers with whom the blossoming of the Western tradition is most often associated—Socrates, Plato, and Aristotle—were, if not always politically motivated, at least always profoundly conscious of the political meaning inherent in every aspect of their thought—not simply their explicitly political or ethical doctrines, but their theories on the nature of the cosmos, or on the nature of human knowledge. The connection between the structure of the cosmos and the organization of the political order in the ideas of both Plato and Aristotle seems clear enough;[1] and in the disputes of Socrates and Plato with the Sophists about the nature of truth and knowledge, one cannot fail to recognize a hierarchical conception of

[1] One commentator has written, for example: "Aristotle wants to show that the Greek city, oligarchical and solidly structured along hierarchical lines, is just because it is constructed in the image of nature. Obviously, this implies that he must have begun to construct nature in the image of the city, . . . and it is by no means easy to distinguish historically what in the politics stems from the science and what in the science stems from the politics." R. Lenoble, "Origines de la pensée scientifique moderne," in *Histoire de la science* (Paris, 1957), p. 391, quoted in Paolo Rossi, *Philosophy, Technology and the Arts in the Early Modern Era* (New York: Harper & Row, 1970), p. 14.

society doing battle with the heritage of Periclean democracy.

It is beyond the scope of this essay to prove that similarly political motivations have affected the course of Western philosophy in more recent times, or to determine—if it is even possible to do so—what came first in any philosophical system. The task here is simply to indicate some affinities, specifically between certain theories of cognition and certain social and political doctrines; and for the sake of simplicity, without asking if the order of presentation reflects or reverses the actual progress of thought in the philosophical systems being examined, the discussion will begin with the cognitive theories and build upon them to the political doctrines. Nevertheless, it may be worth keeping in mind the possibility that sometimes affinities between these different aspects of philosophy may exist precisely because of a tendency—particularly on the part of a supremely political animal like, say, John Locke—to read political life into all experience.[2]

In any case, without pursuing these suggestions any further or making too many claims for the political meaning of all philosophy, it can certainly be said that whatever its source or motivation every conception of man's nature, whether scientific, philosophical, or simply grounded in common sense, has at least potential practical, moral, or even political significance. Concepts of human nature may serve to mark the prudential bound-

---

2 At any rate, one is tempted to suggest that epistemological disputes sometimes revolve around propositions that seem unintelligible, or at best formalistic and scholastic, until they are understood to have some *other* meaning or intention, whether political or otherwise—that is, until they are read as something more than propositions about the nature of cognition. What, for example, does it mean to say that experience is in principle not necessary in the formation of ideas, that experience is simply the "occasion" not the *cause* of ideas? Such a proposition in the case of Descartes (to use an obvious example) might be as much theological as epistemological. It is by formulating his theory of the origin of ideas in a particular way that Descartes is able to make certain statements about the existence of God, who, in the absence of a *direct* relationship between ideas and the world of experience, becomes the cause of the correspondence between ideas and external reality.

aries of human action. Sometimes they may be used as negative standards, dismal portraits of what must be overcome to achieve the morally good life; or they may represent positive moral norms in conjunction with the principle that what is "natural" is "good." Certainly, a conscious or unconscious conception of human nature underlies every choice of social or political values; and there is a common tendency to justify political, social, or economic systems in terms of their supposed conformity to human nature, or to condemn others because of their alleged violations of human nature, their "alienation of man from himself." Moreover, social and political systems tend to institutionalize certain conceptions of man by favoring, rewarding, or placing a premium on certain exemplary human types. Indeed, images of man can be self-fulfilling phophecies. There is nothing unusual, or even particularly controversial, about the observation that people often tend to behave in accordance with the perceptions others have of them. Psychologists, for example, are not infrequently confronted with an inclination on the part of their subjects to adjust their behavior to patterns called for by clinical symptomatology. It may not be so farfetched to imagine, then, that such adjustments take place on a higher, historical plane and that "human nature" may obligingly accommodate itself to the diagnoses of a society's most influential thinkers.

In any case, there comes a point at which analysis of a conception of man ceases to be an empirical problem, a question of the scientific accuracy or viability of that conception, and becomes a practical or even political question. In a sense, it can be argued that ultimately no theory of human nature is empirically verifiable. In the final analysis, whether we approach the problem from the point of view of scientific psychology or philosophical anthropology, we are left with our own perceptions, our own introspection, our own experience of ourselves through which we must interpret our data. Any theory of human nature must in the end be broken down to an irreducible and unverifiable element of self-experience. Sometimes the demands of sci-

entific or linguistic rigor may seem to force us to describe man
in a way which runs counter to our subjective experience of
ourselves. But it can be argued that such descriptions remain
unintelligible until a meaning derived from self-experience is
reintroduced. At any rate, provided there is sufficient "objective" evidence to support the possibility of various conceptions
of man, there is, in the end, little basis for choosing among them.
Aside from empirical verifiability, we have no criterion but our
own self-experience or—and this is the crucial point here—the
practical and moral consequences of adherence to a particular
concept of man. From this point of view, then, we may, after
exhausting all "scientific" evidence available to us at any given
time, find it appropriate to judge theories of man practically
and morally. In other words, it may be useful to ask not only
"What empirical evidence is there for this theory of man?" but
also "What might it mean to act on this image of man?"

This practical dimension is perhaps more apparent in what
we may call the *conative* aspects of conceptions of man—those
which concern human will, desires, passions—than it is in the
cognitive aspects—those which embrace epistemology and conceptions of the mind. Nevertheless, it is the fundamental premise
of this study that moral and even political implications can be
drawn from epistemological theories and their underlying conceptions of the mind; that sometimes, in fact, the ultimate
meaning of a theory of mind may be seen as a moral or political
one; and that sometimes epistemology may, so to speak, be read
as political theory. Again, sometimes theories of epistemology
and conceptions of the mind may seem to establish the groundwork for moral and political doctrines; at times, theories of
mind and epistemology seem instead to be *derived* from moral
or political doctrines. But whichever comes first, the affinities
between theories of mind and political doctrines are often striking, and an examination of those affinities between two perhaps
seemingly unrelated kinds of theory may shed light on the
meaning of both.

Our concern here will be with some social and political implications of the Kantian theory of mind, according to which the
subject plays a positive, in a sense self-active and spontaneously
creative, role in the constitution of experience; and the opposition of this theory to Lockean empiricism, in which the subject
is seen as essentially receptive, reflexive, and responsive—passive
in the sense that it does not play an active role in the constitution
of experience. The link between these theories and political
doctrine will be sought particularly in their common concern
with the problem of human individuality. Perhaps the most
basic questions which must be confronted by social and political
thinkers in some way concern the nature of man's individuality
and his sociality, and the relationship between the two. It is
strange, therefore, that analyses of social and political thought
generally confine themselves to the conative aspects of human
nature as they bear upon the questions of individuality and
sociality, virtually ignoring the importance that a theorist's view
of cognition and the cognitive dimension of the self and individuality may have for social doctrine.

We have begun, then, by opposing the "Kantian" approach
to empiricism; nevertheless, such an opposition may be misleading. Kant certainly did not see his doctrine as diametrically
opposed to philosophical empiricism. If anything, he considered
himself an heir to the empiricists, proceeding from their legacy
in an attempt to correct its deficiencies. It is true that in certain
respects Kant may be said to have sought a synthesis of rational-
ism and empiricism, but it is perhaps more accurate to say that
Kant's epistemology was meant as a correction of empiricism—
a correction that preserved many of the latter's fundamental
principles.[3] In other words, the opposition between the episte-

---

3 Notably, the principle that there are no ideas where there is no sense
experience, and that experience is the cause and the subject matter of ideas,
not simply the occasion—if anything—of ideas, as it is in a sense for the
rationalists. Also, see below, pp. 19–20, for Hegel's account of what Kant
shares with the Lockean empiricists.

mology of Kant and, for example, that of Locke is perhaps an opposition between two kinds of empiricism. The essential character of Kantian "empiricism" and its opposition to Lockean epistemology will be discussed particularly in chapter 1 of this essay, and the implications of these epistemological differences will be developed in subsequent chapters.

The significant point here is that the distinction between these two "empiricisms" can be carried into the realm of social and political thought. Specifically, this distinction has a bearing on the notion of *individualism,* which will be our primary concern in this study. One cannot help being struck, for example, by the coincidence that the British intellectual tradition that contributed so much to the so-called philosophy of individualism should also have fostered the philosophy of empiricism, or by the fact that John Locke, the high priest of empiricism, should also be regarded as a founding father of liberal individualism. Moreover, it is being suggested that, if we can speak of two opposing varieties of empiricism, one exemplified by Locke and his philosophical approach and the other by the Kantian "revolution," an analogous opposition can be found between two modes of individualism; in other words, there is one mode of individualism related to the Kantian approach and another related to the Lockean position.

There is a tendency to apply the term "individualism" rather narrowly to the social doctrine associated with liberal democratic philosophy. In common usage, what purports to be a purely formal objective definition of the term nevertheless secretes certain doctrinal assumptions about the nature of man and society. A number of assumptions are compactly packaged, for example, in the dictionary's opposition of "individualism" to "collectivism," "socialism," etc. Such a definitional antagonism is not justified unless one proceeds from certain liberal premises. If individualism as a social doctrine involves a commitment to the moral primacy of the individual in society and the right of the individual to freedom and self-realization, a host of additional assumptions must be made about man and his relationship to society before "individualism," individual freedom, and self-realization can be made by definition to exclude "socialism" and "collectivism." In short, the meaning of "individualism" depends on one's conception of the nature of individuality.

We have suggested, then, that there are doctrines of individualism which are opposed to Lockean individualism in much the same way that Kantian epistemology is opposed to Lockean empiricism. If this analogy is pursued, insofar as the non-Lockean individualism may encompass "socialism," it can be said that socialism is not the diametric opposite of individualism any more than Kantian epistemology is the opposite of empiricism. The suggestion that Kantian epistemology and the "new" individualism are related is not simply derived by analogy from the relationship between Lockean empiricism and liberal individualism.[4] The connection between the Kantian epistemology and socialist individualism may not be as immediate as that between empiricism and liberal individualism; or at any rate, in the former the union is not so clearly represented in the person of one thinker, as it is in the case of Locke. Nevertheless, it can be argued that socialist individualism, particularly as it is elaborated by Marx, is in a very fundamental sense grounded in or supported by the Kantian philosophical revolution and that Marx derives certain important aspects of his critique of liberalism from principles traceable to the Kantian critique of empirical epistemology.

These connections between theories of mind and social doctrines have a number of aspects, which will be discussed in what

---

4 If Lockean empiricism can, in a sense, be regarded as an "individualistic" epistemology—because of its subjectivism, for example—Kantian epistemology can perhaps be regarded as the ultimate in individualism in a somewhat different sense. See, for example, Georg Simmel's observation that in Kant's philosophy ". . . the ego has wrested its absolute sovereignty. . . . It stands so much on itself alone that even its world, *the* world, can stand on it": *The Sociology of Georg Simmel*, trans. and ed. Kurt Wolff (New York: Free Press, 1964), p. 70.

follows. We can, however, establish a general conceptual framework at the outset by referring to what might be called the *structural* connections between the theories being discussed. One might begin by saying that, in the two cases under scrutiny, each epistemological theory is united to a social theory, not simply by inference, by analogy, or by a concept of man, but by fundamental formal or structural similarities. In other words, they are united by a common mode of thought. The Kantian and Lockean philosophical approaches may be looked upon as representing different modes of thought—or what might be called systems or structures of thought—which have implications for, and manifestations in, a variety of problems which may on the surface seem otherwise unrelated. There are often cases in which a particular mode of thought, a certain form, a system of logic, can be seen as a distinctively characteristic common denominator between, for example, certain scientific theories, on the one hand, and certain philosophical systems, on the other; and this common denominator, this structural similarity, allows one to classify the theories together as representing a single "approach" or "pattern." And for our system of classification perhaps we can adopt in a rather simplified form the Marxist distinction, derived from Hegel, between "metaphysical" and "dialectical" modes of thought.[5]

For our present purpose, we may use Friedrich Engels' characterization of the two modes of thought, with the admission that his presentation of the dialectic is rather superficial and fails to do justice to the philosophical meaning which the concept has for Hegel and even for Marx. If Engels' account is simplistic, it is nonetheless useful here where our intention is simply to outline certain obvious differences in typical patterns of thinking:

5 Hegel distinguishes—for example in the introduction to his *Logic*—between the dialectic and the "older metaphysic." The Marxists—Marx and Engels, later Plekhanov, etc.—refer to the non-dialectical mode of thought simply as the *metaphysical* mode. For the sake of convenience, the latter designation is being adopted here. The special use of the term "metaphysical" will not, I hope, create confusion.

To the metaphysician, things and their mental reflexes, ideas, are isolated, are to be considered one after the other and apart from each other, are objects of investigation fixed, rigid, given once for all. He thinks in absolutely irreconcilable antitheses. "His communication is 'yea, yea; nay, nay'; for whatsoever is more than these cometh of evil." For him a thing either exists or does not exist; a thing cannot at the same time be itself and something else. Positive and negative absolutely exclude one another; cause and effect stand in rigid antithesis one to the other.

. . . And the metaphysical mode of thought, justifiable and necessary as it is in a number of domains . . . sooner or later reaches a limit, beyond which it becomes one-sided, restricted, abstract, lost in insoluble contradictions. In the contemplation of individual things, it forgets the connection between them; in the contemplation of their existence it forgets the beginning and end of that existence; of their repose, it forgets their motion. It cannot see the wood for the trees.

. . . [But] every organic being is every moment the same and not the same . . . every organic being is always itself, and yet something other than itself.

Further, we find upon closer investigation that the two poles of an antithesis, positive and negative, e.g., are as inseparable as they are opposed and that despite all their opposition, they mutually interpenetrate. . . .

None of these processes and modes of thought enters into the framework of metaphysical reasoning. Dialectics, on the other hand, comprehends things and their representations, ideas, in their essential connection, concatenation, motion, origin, and ending.[6]

Engels associates the metaphysical mode of thought with the growth of empirical science, and then, significantly, argues that "this way of looking at things was transferred by Bacon and Locke from natural science to philisophy."[7] Moreover, he goes on to suggest that, at least as far as natural science is concerned, Kant's theory of the solar system marks a crucial breakthrough in the development of dialectics.[8] It can even be argued, as we

6 Friedrich Engels, *Socialism: Utopian and Scientific,* in Karl Marx and Friedrich Engels, *Selected Works* (Moscow: Foreign Language Publishing House, 1962), pp. 130-131.
7 *Ibid.,* p. 130.
8 See, e.g., *Ibid.,* p. 132.

shall see, that it is not simply Kant's scientific thought but his philosophical system as a whole, notably his epistemology, that introduces the dialectic into the "new German philosophy." In fact, it may be suggested that the opposition between the "Kantian" and the "Lockean" approaches corresponds essentially to the Hegelian and Marxist distinction. This would mean that we can speak of Lockean empiricism as "metaphysical" empiricism (remembering that the term "metaphysical" is being used in a special sense), while the Kantian brand of empiricism might be called "dialectical." And, in accordance with our fundamental premise that there is a connection between these epistemological theories and certain social doctrines, perhaps we can also speak of metaphysical and dialectical individualisms.

Thus, for example, if the fundamental characteristics of the dialectical mode of thought are its tendency to reunite rather than simply to separate, to see things in dynamic interaction, to synthesize rather than simply to compare, particularly to unite and synthesize opposites, and, finally, to see things in process rather than static rigidity, we shall see how these qualities are reflected in Kantian epistemology, in its attempt dialectically to unite subject and object. Moreover, it is not difficult to foresee what a dialectical theory of individualism might be. It might, to begin with, take a characteristic view of the relationship between those "antithetical" opposites, individual and society. As we shall see, for example, the dialectical approach, unlike the metaphysical, emphasizes the dynamic unity, the reciprocity, of individual and society, the ways in which individuality and sociality are mutually reinforcing rather than antagonistic. It also conceives of individuality and sociality as evolving through a dialectical interaction in which the nature of self-consciousness and the sense of community develop and mutually change each other in a dynamic process. In any case, the discussion that follows will attempt to show how dialectical individualism reflects both the union of opposites and the dynamic characteristics of the dialectical mode of thought, while metaphysical individualism, in the form of liberalism, maintains the antagonism of opposites and their static rigidity.

Given this general "structural" framework, we can now proceed to a more specific outline of the argument being presented in this essay.

1. The controversy between Kant and the empiricists revolves around the role of the subject in experience—i.e. around the subject-object relation and the question of the independence or "concreteness" of thought and reason.

2. Conceptions of the role of the subject and of the subject-object relation have implications for conceptions of the nature of consciousness and the self, and the relation of self to other—to the external world and other men.

3. These conceptions of the self have a two-fold significance for the present argument:

   i) In their ideas on the relation between the self and the external world in general, they suggest something about the nature of individuality and the freedom of the individual.

   ii) In their ideas on the relation between the self and other men specifically, they suggest something about the relation between the individual and society, individuality and sociality, something about community.

4. Needless to say, ideas on the nature of individuality and sociality, liberty and community, will be reflected in conceptions of man's relation to objective social conditions, and, in particular, the individual's relation to specific social institutions: government, property, etc.

In short, two of the most fundamental political concepts—*liberty* and *community*—can be regarded as two aspects of the self's relation to other. In other words, a conception of the self (and hence, ultimately, a theory of mind) is an implicit unifying factor in political theory—uniting two of its most essential questions; and liberty and community are two sides of the same coin.

I would argue, then, that certain theories of mind and the conceptions of the self they imply tend to encourage or support certain social and political ideas.

To emphasize the connections being suggested here, it may be worth mentioning, in a rather lengthy digression, that the logical associations are at least sufficiently strong actually to have caused a good deal of intellectual uneasiness in the minds of certain thinkers who found themselves holding certain views on the nature of mind and the self, on the one hand, and apparently conflicting social ideas, on the other. David Hume and J. S. Mill are two striking examples.

The problem of the self was an insoluble one for both Hume and Mill, and one which attacked the very foundations of their philosophies. In both instances, the problem is one of reconciling a conception of the mind and the self as simply a "series of feelings, or possibilities of them," with the more definite, independent conception of the self demanded by some of their apparently most cherished principles. Hume in effect admits that his conception of the self cannot sustain his conception of sympathy, the source of community; Mill, that his idea of the self cannot sustain his ideas of individuality and liberty. These ideas of liberty and community seem to be a fundamental source of friction, both within these philosophers' own systems, and often between them and the ideas of their liberal colleagues and predecessors.

The discussion of Hume that appears in chapter 2, for example, cites his attack on Hobbes and Locke for their conceptions of sociality. Hume begins by following Locke's conception of the self to its logical conclusion, but soon finds that it conflicts with his own conception of sympathy. Finally, unable to find a more satisfactory explanation of the self consistent with his philosophical principles, but still unwilling to sacrifice his idea of sympathy, he simply admits his confusion and throws up his hands.

The case with Mill, which is also discussed in what follows, is strikingly similar. It is precisely his conception of individuality and liberty—considered to be his primary innovative contribution to liberalism—that comes into conflict with the rest of his own philosophical system, in which he remains more true to his predecessors. To quote from R. Anschutz's respected work on Mill, in which he discusses Mill's consternation over the difficulties posed by the only theory of Mind and Ego that is compatible with his basic philosophical position:

> In other words, Mill is unable to make anything of the notion of a knowing subject in associationist terms and he is unwilling to try and make anything of it in any other terms. It is hard to imagine a more candid confession of intellectual bankruptcy; and the consequences of Mill's failure in this case are fully as serious as they were in the previous case [i.e., in the case of Mill's account of the objective world. E.W.] For when we turn from speculation to practise, the problem of reconciling flux and permanence in the knowing subject re-emerges as the problem of reconciling determinism and free will in the moral agent; and this is a problem, as Mill had already discovered, which is capable of preying on the mind.[9]

In any case, we may think in terms of two model social theories or two traditions, each characterized primarily by a particular conception of the self-other relationship in both its aspects—that is, particular conceptions of *liberty* and *community*. The model of liberalism is characterized by a conception of liberty in which human freedom is not incompatible with subjection even to objective forces external to the individual; and a conception of community as externalized, perhaps enforced co-existence, assuming atomistic relationships among individuals and, insofar as individuality tends to be equated with atomism and privatization, an essential antagonism between individuality and sociality. The contrasting "Kantian" model is characterized by a conception of freedom as self-activity, autonomy,

[9] R. Anschutz, *The Philosophy of J. S. Mill* (Oxford: Clarendon Press, 1953), pp. 179–180.

and transcendence of objective determination;[10] and a conception of community as an integral part of the human psyche, united in consciousness with individuality, so that sociality and individuality—which here does not simply mean atomism or privatization, but the impulse toward self-activity, creativity, and self-development—are not antagonistic but mutually supportive.[11]

Needless to say, each model will be exemplified by a variety of thinkers whose systems of ideas are not identical to one another. For example, the liberal model or tradition, anticipated by Hobbes, includes Locke, Madison, Bentham, and J. S. Mill. The other group, which is anticipated by Rousseau and includes Kant, Hegel, and Marx, is even more complicated.[12] Since the pivotal point of this essay is the Kantian *revolution,* we must concern ourselves with the "Kantian" model less as the representation of a unified and complete school than as a unified abstraction from a revolutionary *process,* in reaction to the liberal tradition—a process that, in an important sense, begins with Kant's epistemology and culminates in Marx's social theory, proceeding by means of successive adjustments to an initial revolutionary break.[13]

10 The difference between these two conceptions of freedom is perhaps the difference between naturalistic conceptions of man and the conception of man reflected, for example, in Sartre's observation, "What we call freedom is the irreducibility of the cultural order to the natural order": *Search for a Method,* trans. Hazel Barnes (New York: Vintage Books, 1968), p. 152.

11 This distinction between a conception of community as enforced co-existence and a more "integrative" conception of community is reflected in the liberal fascination with punishment and with law and order, in contrast to an opposing view which places less emphasis on violence than on "creative space."

12 Others have sometimes been included, although rather tangentially, for purposes of illustration. Jean Piaget, for example, while he certainly has an elaborate theory of mind, does not explicitly develop a political theory. Nevertheless, his explicit conviction that the natural tendency of the healthy individual, if allowed to mature and develop fully, is toward a desire for equality, autonomy, cooperation, and solidarity with his fellow-men, rather than inequality, heteronomy, competition, and egoism, has some tantalizing implications for political theory, if followed to its logical conclusion.

13 To be perfectly accurate, the object here is not so much to trace the in-

At any rate, as diverse as the thinkers in each group may be, to class them together in this instance seems no less legitimate than in any other instance where thinkers are "lumped together" in either a "school" or a "tradition." To the extent that any school or tradition includes more than one creative thinker, it cannot, of course, be monolithic. The mark of a tradition is surely not identity among its members. Instead, aside from the kinds of "structural" similarities discussed earlier, we tend to bind thinkers together on the basis of a few essential shared assumptions which are so central that the similarities among the thinkers may be regarded as more fundamental than the differences. For example, as has been suggested, the frame of reference in the present discussion is the view that the most salient and far-reaching characteristic of liberalism is its conception of liberty and community; and that all the thinkers here designated as liberals, whatever their specific differences, share these fundamental assumptions about the nature of liberty and community, a fact that places very definite limitations on their specific differences as well. By the same token, the Kantian tradition is united by its opposition to the fundamental assumptions upon which these liberal principles are based.

A more difficult problem is posed by the fact that our "models" unite theories of mind with social and political theories. This means that the models demand a congruity, perhaps even a logical connection, between sets of ideas that are often at best only unconsciously connected in the mind of a given thinker. Perhaps, therefore, it would be useful to emphasize that this essay is seeking to construct something like "ideal types" or

---

fluence of Kant himself as to discuss the significance of a particular theory of mind which is most commonly associated with him. That theory of mind may have been held, and may still be held, by people not influenced by Kant himself, but he is certainly the thinker who is credited with its first systematic elaboration. It seems no less meaningful, then, to designate a certain development in theories of mind as "Kantian" than it is to refer to certain scientific theories as "Newtonian," despite the fact that there may have been scientists who arrived at "Newtonian" insights independently of Newton.

"typological simplifications," which, for purposes of analysis, abstract an integrated, coherent order from the ideas of a number of thinkers who may not themselves have been conscious of such integration, or may not have clearly formulated the implications of their ideas in such a way as to unite them into a coherent system. It is assumed that the construction of such analytical devices is justified, first of all, on the simple grounds that comprehension almost invariably demands an assumption of understandable order. It is in itself significant and illuminating that the material lends itself to the imposition of coherent order by an external observer. It is obviously more significant if there is some indication that the order is not simply a subjective construct imposed by the observer, that the compulsion toward unity and coherence among sets of ideas about different problems is operative within the presumed "tradition" itself. In other words, the use of such typological constructs is particularly useful if the *deviations* from the model which actually occur in concrete cases are, in some sense, "objectively" meaningful. In the present instance, the construction of types seems especially justified, since in those cases where a particular thinker deviates significantly from an ascribed pattern the deviation is objectively meaningful, either in the sense that the thinker himself seems to have felt an imbalance in his system, or in the sense that the deviation is of such a nature that it has triggered a revolution in thought, a "paradigm change," carrying in its wake a series of profound readjustments among various sets of ideas. In other words, in the latter case, a deviation in one element of our pattern seems to have called for, in the minds of immediately succeeding thinkers, a change in the total pattern to restore the balance. If such a relationship, such a compulsion toward balance, consistency, or coherence, seems to exist among sets of ideas about different kinds of problems—for example, between theories of mind and social theories—it seems helpful to think of them as united into a thought pattern or type, whether or not any given thinker reflects the pattern perfectly and consciously.

Here, then, is how the discussion proceeds chapter by chapter. The first chapter begins with a brief discussion of the Kantian "revolution" and its implications for the concept of mind. The central point here is Kant's attribution of a positive, as it were self-active or original, role to the subject in the constitution of experience and the implications this has for the subject-object relation, the dialectical mode of thought, and the concept of freedom.

In chapter 2, the subject-object problem becomes the self-other problem. In other words, the theory of mind and the subject-object dichotomy is pursued to its implications for the idea of consciousness and the self, the process of individuation, the nature of individuality and its relationship to sociality in the development of individual men. Again throughout the discussion an attempt is made to contrast the "Kantian" approach to these problems with the Lockean-empiricist approach.

Chapter 3 proceeds from this examination of the growth of individuality in individual men to an examination of an analogous development in the history of mankind as a whole. In other words, just as chapter 2 deals with the psychological dimension of individuality, chapter 3 discusses the anthropological dimension—the process of individuation in the passage from nature to culture. This discussion then is followed by an analysis of the nature of human sociality and its relationship to individuality and freedom as seen by certain thinkers who reflect the approaches being contrasted.

Chapter 4, on the political dimension of the problem, begins with a few general remarks on the meaning of "individualism" in terms of the different psychological and anthropological conceptions of individuality previously outlined. Finally, an attempt is made to relate these contrasting conceptions of individuality and individualism to Karl Marx's distinction—again inspired by Hegel—between "civil society" and "human society." This distinction, it is held, provides a useful conceptual framework for exemplifying the contrasting princi-

ples of society that might be based respectively on the two contrasting individualisms. In other words, "civil society" might be
the society of metaphysical individualism; "human society,"
that of dialectical individualism.

A few concluding remarks will be devoted to the suggestion
that modern behavioral political science in many fundamental
ways follows in the tradition of the "metaphysical" approach as
here outlined. In a sense, this suggestion constitutes a plea for
the elaboration in modern political theory of a new "antimeta-
physical" approach, as in some ways is already true in other
social sciences.

One final introductory word. It has already been pointed out
that the two "traditions" under discussion are not diametrically
opposed, indeed are in many ways less two traditions than two
aspects of a single one. They are both, after all, "individualisms." The "socialist" mode owes a great deal to the "liberal"
and shares many of its commitments. Only if one forgets this is
it possible to regard a critique of liberalism, such as the one implicit in the present essay, as a betrayal of all the respect for freedom and individuality that liberalism is said to represent. The
present critique is not meant as a betrayal of these "liberal"
values or of the admirable political and legal tradition they reflect, but, on the contrary, simply as a reminder that it is possible
at least to conceive of an "individualism"—perhaps one might
even call it a "liberalism" in a broader sense—that is somewhat
more true to its commitments.

1. The Epistemological Dimension: Subject and Object

> The true dialectic is not a monologue of a solitary thinker
> with himself; it is a dialogue between I and thou.
>
> LUDWIG FEUERBACH
> *Principles of the Philosophy of the Future*

The Kantian Revolution: The Active Mind and Dialectical Empiricism

That Kant marks a revolution in the history of philosophy seems to be generally recognized, but in what that revolution consists is often not so clear. It is well known that Kant began with an attempt to solve the problem bequeathed to him by Hume—the problem of the origin of our concept of cause and effect, given that it cannot be deduced from experience—and ended by concluding that this concept and, moreover, many other categories which are indispensable to thought "were not deduced from experience, as Hume had apprehended, but sprang from the pure understanding."[1] What, however, is the significance of this conclusion that the fundamental categories of thought are supplied by the mind a priori to experience? One of the most explicit interpretations of Kant's contribution to the "new philosophy" comes from the greatest philosopher of the new tradition, Hegel. In his *Lectures on the History of Philosophy*, Hegel summarizes the Kantian breakthrough by pointing out that, although Kant proceeds from the empiricist tradition, in a sense sharing with philosophers like Locke and Hume the denial of universality and necessity in perception, he works a fundamental change in that empiricist principle. While the

[1] Immanuel Kant, *Prolegomena to Any Future Metaphysics*, ed. Paul Carus (La Salle, Ill.: The Open Court Publishing Company, 1955), Kant's Introduction, p. 7.

empiricists attack the universality and necessity of the categories in general,

> Kant merely argues against their objectivity in so far as they are present in external things themselves, while maintaining them to be objective in the sense of holding good as universal and necessary, as they do for instance in mathematics and natural science. . . . But if universality and necessity do not exist in external things, the question arises "Where are they to be found?" To this Kant, as against Hume, maintains that they must be *a priori*, i.e., that they must rest on reason itself, and on thought as self-conscious reason: their source is the subject, "I" in my self-consciousness. This, simply expressed, is the main point in the Kantian philosophy.[2]

The Kantian revolution has a number of profound implications which may not be apparent at first glance. The most obvious, as important as it may be, is perhaps not the most significant, as Hegel's subsequent discussion reveals. It is undoubtedly significant that Kant, while retaining the empiricist emphasis on the subject, the self, the individual, replaces the solipsism—the radical individualism, if you will—that he seems to feel is inherent in empiricist epistemology, with a kind of universifiable, "objective" subjectivity. But the subject undergoes other and even more fundamental transformations. The fact that the subject in effect constitutes, creates, "legislates," objectivity not only implies a different meaning for subjectivity and objectivity; it also reflects a different conception of the role of the subject in experience. Kant's subject no longer has simply the passive, responsive, reflexive role inherent in the empiricist concept of mind. The mind is conceived by Kant as self-active, in a sense autonomous; the subject is a positive, creative participant in the construction of experience. Passive reflections and associations are replaced by active synthesis. As Hegel says:

> Kant considers thought as in great measure a synthetic activity. . . . Since Kant shows that thought has synthetic judgments *a priori*

2 G. W. F. Hegel, *Lectures on the History of Philosophy*, trans. E. S. Haldane and Frances H. Simson (London: Routledge and Kegan Paul, 1955), III, 427–428.

which are not derived from perception he shows that thought is so to speak concrete in itself.[3]

This distinction between the "active" mind of Kant's doctrine and the "passive" mind of classical empiricism must be clarified, especially since the terms "active" and "passive" are often used somewhat indiscriminately and not very consistently by the thinkers themselves in their own accounts of the mind's role in knowledge. In any case, some kind of "activity" at some stage in the process of knowing can be attributed to the mind in any theory of knowledge. In this essay, however, the terms are being used in a rather specific sense. The reference here is to the nature of experience itself and to the role of the subject in experience, not simply to what subsequently happens to the data of experience. In other words, the mind is called active or passive according to its original role in the creation of the basic constituents of knowledge.

The point of empiricism is precisely that experience is, so to speak, given. Experience is the receiving of impressions involving the direct action of object on subject. The mind may subsequently be "active" in comparing, combining, etc., the data of experience, but in its original relation to the material of knowledge, the subject is passive and receptive. Moreover, even the subsequent mental activity whereby more complex ideas are formed from experience in a sense simply involves drawing out what is already given in the object (e.g. deriving ideas of space and time from a particular objective association or conjunction of certain sense impressions). To quote Hegel on Locke:

Locke, however, places the reality of the understanding only in the formal activity of constituting new determinations from the simple conceptions received by means of perception, through their comparison and combination of several into one; it is the apprehension of the abstract sensations which are contained in the objects.[4]

3 *Ibid.*, p. 430.
4 *Ibid.*

According to Locke, for example, the ideas of time and space are themselves derived from perception; they are, in essence, externally given and received as experience:

> I have showed above, chapter four, that we get the idea of space, both by our sight and touch; which, I think, is so evident that it would be as needless to go to prove that men perceive, by their sight, a distance between bodies of different colours, or between the parts of the same body, as that they see colours themselves.[5]

In effect, the mind derives general ideas of time and space from perceptions of particular time sequences or spatial relations. Hegel even argues that Locke's formulation is an empty tautology: "Since distance itself is really space, mind thus determines space from space."[6]

The Kantian position is opposed to classical empiricism not because of the importance the latter attaches to experience, but because of its conception of the nature of experience itself and the role of the subject in experience. In brief, the Kantian argument is that the subject is active in the constitution of experience itself. The subject does not simply *receive* experience; it creates and constructs it. The "object" is not simply something that is independently given, a "primary datum," to be imposed on the subject as is; instead, "objectivity" is the product of the subject's activity.

Kant's doctrine of the "active" mind is reflected in his distinction between *perception* and *experience*. The former involves simply passive reception by the senses; the latter, the objectifica-

---

5 John Locke, *An Essay Concerning Human Understanding*, ed. Alexander Campbell Fraser (New York: Dover Publications, 1959), I, 219 (Bk. II, chap. xiii, art. 2). Hereafter referred to as *Essay*.

6 Hegel, *op. cit.*, p. 306. Kant's conception is, of course, well known. The principles of time and space are not simply derived from experience. On the contrary, they are a priori contributions of the mind to experience. The mind constructs experience by applying a priori synthetic judgments to sense data. To quote Hegel again: "Since Kant shows that thought has synthetic judgments *a priori* which are not derived from perception, he shows that thought is so to speak concrete in itself" (*ibid.*, p. 430). The synthetic activity of mind occurs, in other words, at the most elementary level of experience.

tion of perception through the synthetic, original activity of the understanding:

> We must consequently analyse experience in order to see what is contained in this product of the senses and of the understanding, and how the judgement of experience itself is possible. . . .
> Before, therefore, a judgement of perception can become a judgement of experience, it is requisite that the perception should be subsumed under some such a *(a priori)* concept of the understanding. . . . [Kant's note: I add to the perception a concept of the understanding . . . and the synthetical judgement becomes of necessity universally valid, viz., objective, and is converted from a perception into experience.][7]

In another work, Kant expresses the same idea:

> Experience is an empirical knowledge, that is, a knowledge which determines an object through perceptions. It is a synthesis of perceptions, not contained in perception but itself containing in one consciousness the synthetic unity of the manifold of perceptions. This synthetic unity constitutes the essential in any knowledge of *objects* of the senses, that is, in experience as distinguished from mere intuition or sensation of the senses.[8]

Thus, again, the *object*—the objectivity of perception, which is experience—is created by the subject, and not simply given. Kant clearly regards this idea as the crux of his opposition to the empiricists—that is, significantly, to *both* Locke and Hume. It is important to note, too, that, whatever the differences Kant may see between Locke and Hume, these differences do not lie in what he considers to be the most fundamental principles of their conceptions of the mind:

> The illustrious Locke, failing to take account of these considerations, and meeting with pure concepts of the understanding in experiences, deduced them also from experience, and yet proceeded so *inconsequently* that he attempted with their aid to obtain knowledge which far transcends all limits of experience. David Hume recognizes that, in order to be able to do this, it was necessary that these con-

7 Kant, *op. cit.*, pp. 57–59.
8 Kant, *Critique of Pure Reason*, trans. Norman Kemp Smith (New York: St. Martin's Press, 1965), p. 209.

cepts should have an *a priori* origin. But since he could not explain how it can be possible that the understanding must think concepts, which are not in themselves connected in the understanding, as being necessarily connected in the object, and since it never occurred to him that the understanding might itself, perhaps, through these concepts, be the author of the experience in which its objects are found, he was constrained to derive them from experience, namely, from a subjective necessity (that is, from *custom*), which arises from repeated association in experience, and which comes mistakenly to be regarded as objective.[9]

In short, the difference between Hume and Locke does not rest, according to Kant, on any fundamental disagreement concerning the nature of experience, the nature of objectivity, the original activity of mind, or the role of the subject in the creation of the constituents of knowledge. Instead, the difference is simply a result of Locke's failure to see the ultimate implications of his own theory of mind, while Hume confronts these implications. Since, however, Hume tries to deal with the implications without fundamentally altering the basic conception of mind, he is himself dissatisfied with the result.

In assessing the significance of Kant's doctrine and his objections to empiricism, it is interesting to note, to begin with, that his most influential successors—for example, Hegel and *his* heirs —have chosen to emphasize that aspect of Kant's argument establishing the spontaneity, creativity, and freedom of reason, rather than to stress the rigidity and determinism some may see in the notion of a priori categories.[10] In Kant's defense of the possibility of synthetic a priori judgments and his contention that experience, the basic material of knowledge, is not simply given but created, they have seen the "rescue of reason from the empirical onslaught,"[11] the restoration of reason as a free, creative force—in fact, an affirmation of human freedom and man's transcendence. It seems clear, moreover, that Kant himself believed

9 *Ibid.*, p. 127.
10 See for example, pp. 43–44, below.
11 Herbert Marcuse, *Reason and Revolution*, 2nd ed. (New York: Humanities Press, 1954), p. 23.

he was establishing the spontaneous creativity of the mind and in so doing affirming the possibility of human freedom and genuine moral choice. For him, understanding was the principle of *spontaneity* (the "determinative"), while sensibility was the principle of *receptivity* the ("determined"): ". . . synthesis is an expression of spontaneity, which is determinative and not, like sense, determinable merely. . . ." [12] Moreover, this original "spontaneity" is the basis of all subsequent expressions of such freedom:

> This synthesis is an action of the understanding on the sensibility, and is its first application—and thereby the ground of all its other applications—to the objects of our possible intuition. [13]

There is, however, more to Kant's revision of empirical epistemology and its implications for the problem of freedom. In his discussion of freedom, Kant makes it quite clear that for him the question is not simply one of transferring causality from a source external to the individual to an internal source, nor is it even simply a matter of rational causes prevailing over other internal, nonrational impulses. An immediate internal cause, whether rational or instinctual, may still be part of an endless causal chain and still be determined by antecedent causes, while *freedom* demands spontaneity, or "causality through freedom," the *beginning* of a causal series. In spite of Kant's distinction between "practical" and "transcendental" freedom, and his definition of the former as the independence of will from sensuous impulse, he emphasizes that ultimately an act is *not* free simply because it issues from a rational impulse rather than from blind instinct or from an immediate response to external stimuli. Indeed, in the final analysis, transcendental freedom or "absolute spontaneity" is the only "proper" freedom, and even practical freedom has no meaning except as "transcendental":

> In the question of freedom which lies at the foundation of all moral laws and accountability to them, it is really not at all a question of

12 Kant, *Critique, op. cit.*, p. 165.
13 *Ibid.*

whether the causality determined by a natural law is necessary through determining grounds lying within or without the subject, or whether, if they lie within him, they are in instinct or in grounds of determination thought by reason . . . they also imply natural necessity, leaving no room for transcendental freedom. . . . Without transcendental freedom, which is its proper meaning, and which is alone *a priori* practical, no moral law and no accountability to it are possible.[14]

The implications for freedom that Kant attributes to his theory of the active mind, then, would seem to be more subtle and complex than they appear at first. In light of his argument that more is required to meet the criteria of freedom than rational determination alone, Kant's conception of the active mind might be interpreted as supplying the missing ingredient that makes practical freedom "transcendental." In other words, one might simply take Kant to be saying that rational determination is not enough if reason itself is an essentially passive and derivative phenomenon; and that freedom requires not only that a given act have its immediate source in reason, but that reason be in principle a creative and spontaneous force—a force more "free" than the prudence of Hobbesian man, the slave, albeit "enlightened," of the passions, capable only of deferring fulfillment of pleasure. It would seem that Kant's rejection of this conception of reason might by itself distinguish his idea of practical freedom from the "quibbling," the "wretched subterfuge" he attributes to the empiricist doctrine of freedom and its attempts to reconcile freedom and causality.

Kant, however, is not satisfied to rest his argument on the simple assertion that the mind is a "determinative," spontaneous principle that can "constitute" objects. Having argued that the only "proper meaning" of freedom even in its practical sense is transcendental spontaneity, he tries to find a basis in *experience*, and not simply in logic, for belief in the possibility of transcendental freedom. This experiential basis he finds in the

---

[14] Kant, *Critique of Practical Reason*, trans. Lewis White Beck (Indianapolis: Bobbs-Merrill Co., 1956), pp. 99–100.

moral experience, the feeling of "ought." This experience ultimately depends upon man's consciousness of himself through
"pure apperception," not simply through momentary sense impressions, and his consciousness of himself as "thing-in-itself,"
transcending the causal order of nature. Man, insofar as he is
conscious of himself as a "thing-in-itself,"

> . . . also views his existence so far as it does not stand under temporal
> conditions, and himself as determinable only by laws which he gives
> to himself through reason. In this existence nothing is antecedent to
> the determination of his will; every action, and, in general, every
> changing determination of his existence according to the inner sense,
> even the entire history of his existence as a sensuous being, is seen in
> the consciousness of his intelligible existence as only a consequence,
> not as a determining ground of his causality as noumenon.[15]

In other words, only in the case of his own consciousness of self
does man have experiental "evidence" of anything existing, not
only as conditioned phenomenon, but also as "noumenon" capable of standing outside, and originating, a causal chain.[16]

---

[15] *Ibid.*, p. 101.

[16] Kant's remarks to the effect that man as noumenon is free, but as phenomenon is part of the casual order of nature, have often caused a great deal
of consternation. Even Kant's admirers often seem to feel that this position
requires elaborate and subtle defense. Why this proposition should be so
disturbing is not always clear. It is as if Kant were suggesting that man is in
fact part of a rigid causal mechanism, and that whatever "freedom" he has
is somehow bogus or illusory, and his ability to "think" freedom is hardly
better than self-deception or, at best, mental gymnastics. If some such interpretation is at the root of the discomfort that Kant sometimes causes, then
it would seem that this discomfort arises out of a failure to keep in mind the
framework within which Kant is always operating in the *Critiques*. Whatever the ambiguities in Kant's formulation, one thing is clear enough: Kant
does not claim to be writing about the attributes of the "real" world as such,
but simply about the nature of man's cognition and experience of that
world. It is simply not his intention in the *Critiques* to discourse on the
"laws of nature," either in general or as they operate on man. It seems
hardly necessary to argue that Kant is here interested in the principle of
causality, not as an attribute of things, but simply as the way in which men
experience uniformity and encompass contiguous events in one unified experience. If he sometimes expresses himself in a manner that suggests something more, it is nevertheless clear that everything he says must be understood within the terms of his original frame of reference. Kant himself indicates that his sometimes confusing use of linguistic conventions—his refer-

It is in this connection that Kant's theory of mind and cognition plays another crucial, if subtle and indirect, role in his doctrine of freedom. As we shall see later, Kant in his epistemology has carefully laid the foundation for a new theory of self-consciousness which, as much as any other aspect of his philosophy, distinguishes him from his empiricist predecessors. This theory, which depends upon his conception of the active mind, tries to account for the sense of self that men experience as a constant, positive theme of the mind, while the empiricists can describe the self as nothing more than that awareness accompanying each fleeting sense impression. Kant's epistemology may not satisfactorily explain or "verify" this experience of the self which is so central to his doctrine of freedom, but his theory at least makes it possible to recognize it philosophically, to in-

---

ences to "laws of causality" or the "nature of things"—is still to be understood as a comment on the nature of cognition and experience. Consider, for example: "The proposition that nothing happens through blind chance . . . is therefore an *a priori* law of nature. So also is the proposition that no necessity in nature is blind, but always a conditioned and therefore intelligible necessity. . . . Both are laws through which the play of alterations is rendered subject to a nature of things (that is, of things as appearances), *or what amounts to the same thing, to the unity of understanding, in which alone they can belong to one experience, that is, to the synthetic unity of appearances*" (*Critique of Pure Reason, op. cit.*, p. 248: emphasis in the last sentence added).

The significant point is that, while in the case of our knowledge of external events we can add nothing to this mode of experience—this knowledge of things under the principle of causality, that is, as phenomena—in the case of our own self-knowledge we are capable of a different mode of experience—the experience of ourselves as spontaneous agents, which has been discussed above. Moreover, the "evidence" supplied by this form of "experience," if different in its mode of representation, is no less "certain" than empirical evidence. In short, the very least that can be said is that, given Kant's essential frame of reference, there is nothing in his distinction between man as noumenon and man as phenomenon that suggests that the experience of freedom is any more false or deceptive than the experience of causality.

There is perhaps more ground for uneasiness in what Kant *failed* to do than in what he did in elaborating his doctrine of freedom; and it is tempting to argue that it is precisely the challenge of completing his conception of freedom that was taken up by thinkers like Marx, who attempts to give concrete expression to Kant's notion of freedom as self-activity—a point that will be discussed further in what follows.

corporate it into his system. Again, as we shall see, it is precisely this experience of the self as a constant theme of the mind that makes both Hume and Mill so uneasy when they try to give an account of the self on the basis of principles inherited from Locke. They are uneasy because, while they are themselves conscious of such an experience, their own theories of mind seem to render the experience impossible or at least absurd. Both of them simply disown the experience philosophically, while reluctantly admitting it "privately." Kant, however, must make this experience of the self an integral part of his system, since it provides the "proof" of freedom. He must therefore revise empiricist epistemology precisely at the point where it denies the possibility of this distinctive sense of self.

In effect, then, Kant's epistemology is the basis of his moral doctrine, since, to establish man's "transcendental spontaneity" and the possibility of self-active, conscious rational choice, Kant must first show that reason asserts primacy in its most important confrontation with the external world—in experience itself—not only because of what this says directly about the "freedom" of reason, but because of what it says more indirectly about the nature of the self. His attack on the empiricists, therefore, is not simply an epistemological quibble, but a far-reaching argument about the nature of human freedom.

Another point must be emphasized in examining the significance of Kant's argument, with particluar reference to his distinction between perception and experience. In terms of the actual psychology of the individual mind—as distinct from the archetypal epistemology of the model mind—Kant sees the relationship between perception and experience as, in part, a developmental one. The human infant first *perceives* and only subsequently *experiences*. The capacity for experience is achieved, the understanding is activated, through increasing confrontations with the external world:

> The fact that during this period [of infancy] it [the child] begins to follow shiny objects with its eyes marks the crude beginning of the

progress of perceptions (apprehension of the representation of sensation), expanding them into knowledge of the objects of sense, that is, experience.[17]

And further on:

Remembrance of one's childhood does not reach back nearly to that time, however, since it was not the time of experience, but simply of scattered perceptions not yet united in the conception of the object.[18]

The significance of these ideas for Kant's conception of the self—in a discussion of which the passages just cited actually appear—will be explored in the next chapter. For the moment, a further point that arises out of the foregoing discussion bears mentioning. It has perhaps already become apparent that a central theme of Kant's doctrine is the reunification of subject and object. For example, his conception of experience in a sense lessens the rigid opposition between subject and object implied by the theory of empiricism. In the latter, the object is an independently existing *given,* standing over and against the subject; while for Kant, the object is itself the product of subjective creativity and the active interpenetration of the subject and the external world.[19] Again, Kant's developmental conception of the

17 Kant, *Anthropologie in pragmatischer Hinsicht,* in *Gesammelte Schriften* (Berlin: Prussian Academy of Sciences, 1917), VII, 127–128: "Das es in diesem Zeitraum ihm vorgehaltenen glänzenden Gegenständen mit Augen zu folgen anhebt, ist der rohe Anfang des Fortschreitens von Wahrnehmungen (Apprehension der Empfindungsvorstellung), um sie zum Erkenntnis der Gegenstände der Sinne, d.i. der Erfahrung, zu erweitern." (The original text is included when the translation is my own. E.W.)
18 *Ibid.,* p. 128. "Die Erinnerung seiner Kinderjahre reicht aber bei weitem nicht bis an jene Zeit, weil sie nicht die Zeit der Erfahrungen, sondern bloss zerstreuter, unter den Begriff des Objects noch nicht vereinigter Wahrnehmungen war."
19 It is left in part to Hegel and finally to Marx, whose contribution to this question will be discussed in the next section, to treat the problem of the subject-object relation as a problem of existence and not simply of epistemology, and to find the ultimate reunification of subject and object in the unification of thought and existence through human practice. Marx's reformulation of the problem emphasizes even more strikingly the implications of the Kantian revolution for conceptions of human freedom and social life.

relationship between perception and experience emphasizes the dynamic interaction of the subject and external reality, self and other. For Hegel, this conception of the subject-object relation has a special significance, because he sees in it the principle of the dialectic. The dialectic, with few exceptions long absent from philosophy, has thus been reintroduced into the "new" German philosophy through Kant's system of thought:

> . . . besides the general idea of synthetic judgments *a priori,* a universal which has difference in itself, Kant's instinct carried this out in accordance with the scheme of triplicity, unspiritual though that was, in the whole system into which for him the entire universe was divided. This he not only practised on the three critiques, but he also followed it out in most of the subdivisions under the categories, the ideas of Reason, etc. Kant has therefore set forth as a universal scheme the rhythm of knowledge, of scientific movement; and has exhibited on all sides thesis, antithesis and synthesis, modes of mind by means of which it is mind, as thus consciously distinguishing itself. The first is existence, but in the form of Other-Being for consciousness; for what is only existence is object. The second is Being-for-self, genuine actuality; here the reverse relation enters in, for self-consciousness, as the negative of Being-in-itself, is itself relative. The third is the unity of the two: the absolute self-conscious actuality is the sum of true actuality, into which are reabsorbed both the objective and the independently existent subjective. Kant has thus made an historical statement of the moments of the whole, and has correctly determined and distinguished them: it is a good introduction to philosophy.[20]

The Kantian revolution from this point of view is essentially the re-establishment of the dialectic in philosophy by means of a certain conception of the relation between subject and object, self and other. It is not only the dialectical mode of thought that is significant here, but the fact that the basis of the dialectic, the dialectic in its very essence, is a relationship between self and other. It will be seen that this form of the dialectic may have profound implications for conceptions of society. It is not difficult to see, for example, how epistemology is translated into

20 Hegel, *op. cit.,* pp. 477–478.

social theory when one considers how the epistemological subject is transformed by Marx into "man as a human and natural
subject endowed with eyes, ears, etc., and living in society, in the
world, and in nature."[21] The activity of mind becomes practical
activity; the relationship between self and other becomes the
social relations between man and man when Marx, like Feuerbach, proceeds from the principle that "the true dialectic is not
a monologue of a solitary thinker; it is a dialogue between I
and thou."[22]

To sum up the implications of the discussion so far, then, it
can be said that, by affirming the creative self-activity of the subject and the spontaneous independence of reason, and by re-
establishing the dialectic, particularly with reference to the
subject-object relation and the unity of self and other, the Kantian revolution, as we shall see more clearly in what follows, lays
the groundwork for a transformation of the self-other problem
in both its aspects: the self-other relation as the problem of liberty and as the problem of community.

The Self-Active Subject Becomes the Free Man

The implications for social theory of the Kantian concept of
mind may become more immediate and striking if one considers
what Marx does to this concept, how he transforms it quite consciously and directly into a theory of society and social action.

That Marx belongs to the Kantian tradition may not be immediately apparent. In fact, interpretations of Marxist materialism very often suggest precisely the kind of passive empiricism—
and that in an extreme form—to which the Kantian theory of
mind is opposed. This materialism is often understood to imply
that human consciousness is simply a passive product, a mere
reflection of objective material conditions; and this conception

---

21 Karl Marx, "Critique of the Hegelian Dialectic and Philosophy as a
Whole," in *Economic and Philosophic Manuscripts of 1844*, trans. M. Milligan, ed. Dirk J. Struik (New York: International Publishers, 1964), p. 191.
22 Ludwig Feuerbach, *Principles of the Philosophy of the Future*, trans. M.
H. Vogel (Indianapolis: Bobbs-Merrill Co., 1966), art. 62, p. 72.

of consciousness is presumed to lie at the heart of the crude determinism often attributed to Marx.

In fact, however, Marx quite explicitly attacks this kind of deterministic materialism; and it is precisely because he sides with idealism in its opposition to the passive determinism of empiricism—which lies at the heart of the eighteenth-century materialism he is attacking—that he is able to translate his epistemology into a theory of society, social action, and revolution. The *Theses on Feuerbach* clearly demonstrates how Marx seeks to elaborate a theory of mind into a social doctrine. In the first place, he expands the idea of mental activity proposed by idealism into a concept of practical activity. Moreover, in so doing, he also gives concrete social form to the dialectical relationship between subject and object by making it a principle of social relations. In Theses IX and X, he rather mysteriously associates the old materialism with a particular principle of society—"civil society"—and suggests that the new materialism will be the basis of a new social principle, the principle of "human society." He is here quite explicitly connecting certain epistmological theories with certain conceptions of society.[23] The latter connections will be discussed in greater detail in the final chapter. For the moment, while we are still examining epistemology, more needs to be said about Marx's relation to the Kantian tradition, particularly since he is so often misunderstood on this score.

Marx begins the *Theses on Feuerbach* by attacking earlier theories of materialism and opposing to their objective determinism an emphasis on what might be called the principle of

23 If we adopt the popular designation of Marxist philosophy as "dialectical materialism," perhaps we can add another dimension to the meaning of that term. If Kant's theory of mind can be called "dialectical empiricism," as has been suggested, perhaps the Marxist theory can be interpreted as a transformation of this principle into a concrete social theory. "Dialectical materialism," then, would involve a concept of society based on the practically active subject—i.e. creative man—and the practical reunification of subject and object, self and other, at all levels—for example, the reunification of man with his own previously alienated activity, man with man, the individual with his social powers.

subjectivity and the idea of subjective activity introduced by idealism.

> The chief defect of all previous materialism (including that of Feuer-bach) is that things (*Gegenstand*), reality, the sensible world, are conceived only in the form of *objects* (*Objekt*) of *observation,* but not as *human sense activity,* not as *practical activity,* not subjectively. Hence, in opposition to materialism, the *active* side was developed abstractly by idealism, which of course does not know real sense activity as such.[24]

In a very fundamental sense, this emphasis on the principle of subjectivity is the essence of Marx's philosophy. Implicit in it is his idea of freedom as self-activity, self-creation, and individual self-realization—the reunification of subject and object by means of man's active participation in the world through use of all his faculties. The condition for this freedom is man's conscious transcendence and practical mastery of objective reality. All previous materialism, with its empiricist epistemological base, is a denial of human subjectivity and individuality in the sense that it must regard man simply as an object, as a passive, receptive function of objective conditions. In idealism Marx sees a basis for rejecting the untranscendable determinism of early materialism and for establishing the principle that man as free conscious subject can and must transcend his passive determination by objective reality and historical forces. This is what it means to leave the stage of prehistory and enter the stage of true human history. Marx's social, political, and economic theories are, as it were, statements of the conditions necessary to achieve "subjectivity"—that is, to achieve mastery over objects and attain self-realization through the practical reunification of subject and object.

Marx proceeds, then, from the idealist attempt to bridge the

---

24 Marx, *Theses on Feuerbach,* in Karl Marx, *Selected Writings in Sociology and Social Philosophy,* ed. T. B. Bottomore and M. Rubel (Harmondsworth: Penguin Books, 1963), Thesis I, p. 82.

gap between subject and object. However, as he indicates in the statement cited above, he is not entirely satisfied with the idealist attempt, because idealism remains in the abstract realm of mental activity and fails to deal with man as he is in the world, as active participant in life and society. The epistemological re-unification of subject and object can, in fact, be achieved only through man's, the subject's, active participation in objective reality. Only to the degree that man, having consciously grasped reality, can *change* reality—and through it, himself—can one really say that the chasm between subject and object has been closed and that the principle of subjectivity and individuality has prevailed. Having added this practical dimension to the old epistemological problem, Marx argues that he renders irrelevant the difficulty that still plagued the idealists, notably Kant, in their attempts to bridge the gap between subject and object. Kant, for example, still retained the gap insofar as he questioned the accessibility of ultimate reality to human thought and knowledge. For Marx, the "reality" of thought is no longer a problem, if man himself can change reality—and change it in accordance with his conscious goals. The ability to change reality in accordance with human thought is practical proof of the truth of thought. The unity of theory and practice can mean the unity of subject and object.

> The question whether human thinking can pretend to objective *(gegenständlich)* truth is not a theoretical but a *practical* question. Man must prove the truth, i.e., the reality and power, the "this-sideness" of his thinking in practise. The dispute over the reality or non-reality of thinking that is isolated from practise is purely a *scholastic* question.[25]

Marx has thus elaborated on the Kantian theory of mind by proposing revolutionary practice as a new form of consciousness, and the theory of mind has become a social doctrine. As Shlomo

25 *Ibid.*, Thesis II, p. 82.

Avineri puts it, "Revolutionary *praxis* is an active and social epistemology."[26] We shall see later how Marx develops this theme.

At this point it must be emphasized that the determinism that Marx is attacking, and its implicit conception of freedom as compatible with determination even by external objective forces, does not belong simply to the frankly mechanistic, deterministic doctrines of uncompromising materialists like Hobbes, but to the more "liberal" systems of his successors as well. Moreover, this conception of freedom is reflected not only indirectly in liberal doctrines of social and political liberty, which will be discussed in subsequent chapters, but in the more fundamental philosophical principles that underlie them. This point can be illustrated by considering the very thinkers who would seem to pose the most serious challenge to this argument: Locke and J. S. Mill.

According to Locke, for example, the freedom of the agent lies, to begin with, in the absence of impediments to action determined by the will—not in the "freedom" of volition itself.

> So that liberty is not an idea belonging to volition, or preferring; but to the person having the power of doing, or forbearing to do, according as the mind shall choose or direct. Our idea of liberty reaches as far as that power, and no farther. For wherever restraint comes to check that power, or compulsion takes away that indifferency of ability to act, or to forbear acting, there liberty, and our notion of it, presently ceases.[27]

---

26 Shlomo Avineri, *The Social and Political Thought of Karl Marx* (Cambridge: Cambridge University Press, 1968), p. 149. Avineri also provides a convincing explanation of Marx's well-known observation that "it is not the consciousness of men that determines their being, but, on the contrary, their social being determines their consciousness"—an observation often understood to contradict the interpretation of Marx being presented here. Avineri writes: " 'Social being' includes by definition man's relation to the external world, and the worst that can be said about this much-quoted and little-understood sentence is that it is tautological. If 'social being' is purposive action, the shaping of external objects, this action implies a consciousness in relation to these external objects. In any case, Marx never said that 'being determines consciousness', but that '*social* being determines consciousness': these are two entirely different statements" (*ibid.*, pp. 75–76).

27 Locke, *Essay*, p. 317 (Bk. II, chap. xxi, art. 10).

Thus, I think, first, that so far as anyone can, by the direction or choice of his mind, preferring the existence of any action to the non-existence of that action, and *vice versa,* make *it* to exist or not exist, so far *he* is free.[28]

Up to this point, it is clear that freedom lies in the absence of impediment to voluntary motion, but that the will itself is quite mechanistically determined. The opposite of "voluntary" is not "necessary," but simply "involuntary."[29] In the first edition of the *Essay,* Locke leaves it at that.

In the second edition, *without* removing the passages which speak of freedom as absence of restraint of voluntary action, no matter how mechanistically determined volition itself may be, Locke adds another element to his definition of freedom which may seem to suggest that voluntary action is not entirely mechanistically determined. This is the notion that the mind can *"suspend* the execution and satisfaction of any of its desires," [30] and that freedom lies in this power of suspension. The "uneasiness" which *almost* always determines the will to action need not *always* do so.

The difficulty, however, is that Locke provides no explanation of this power to suspend volition. This idea, if taken at face value, is contradicted by everything that goes before it—everything Locke says about desires, volition, the nature of the self, and, more fundamentally, about the mind and its role in experience—which provides no basis for a truly independent act of mind. On the basis of Locke's own premises, one can only conclude that this suspension itself is a determined act of volition. As A. C. Fraser puts it in his notes to the *Essay*:

> But unless in this man rises above a merely natural causation of motives, he is no more ethically free in suspending voluntary execution of a desire than in any other exercise of will. A power to suspend volition, necessarily thus dependent, leaves man still a part of the mechanism of nature.

28 *Ibid.,* p. 324 (art. 21).
29 See *ibid.,* p. 318 (art. 11).
30 *Ibid.,* p. 345 (art. 48).

. . . after all, on his premises, the suspension must be the natural issue of uneasiness.[31]

A particularly forceful attack on Locke's conception of freedom and moral responsibility comes, interestingly enough, from T. H. Green. It is worth quoting at some length from Green's remarks, because they illuminate the present argument by attributing the difficulties in Locke's doctrine precisely to empiricism's denial of the "originativeness of thought" and to its inability to account for the *self* as anything more than a discontinuous series of sensations or the simple awareness that accompanies individual perceptions.[32] Here then is Green's argument:

. . . the "suspense of desire," that he speaks of, can only mean an interval, during which a competition of imagined pleasure (one associated with more, another with less, of sequent or antecedent pain) is still going on, and none has become finally the strongest motive. Of such suspense it is unmeaning to say that a man has "the power of it," or that, when it terminates in an action which does not produce so much pleasure as another might have done, it is because the man "has vitiated his palate," and that therefore he must be "answerable to himself" for the consequences. This language really implies that pleasures, instead of being ultimate ends, are determined to be ends through reference to an object beyond them which the man himself constitutes; that it is only through his conception of self that every pleasure—not indeed best pleases him, or is most attractive in imagination—but becomes his personal good.

. . . Thus when Locke finds the ground of responsibility in man's power of suspending his desire 'till he has considered whether the act, to which it inclines him, is of a kind to make him happy or no, the value of the explanation lies in the distinction which it may be taken to imply, but which Locke could not consistently admit, between the imagination of pleasure and the conception of self as a permanent subject of happiness, by reference to which an imagined pleasure becomes a strongest motive.

. . . This ambiguous deliverance about moral freedom, it must be observed, is the necessary result, on a mind having too strong a prac-

---

31 *Ibid.*, p. 345, nn. 1 and 2.
32 See below, pp. 49–51, for a more detailed discussion of the empiricist conception of the self.

tical hold on life to tamper with human responsibility, of a doctrine which denies the originativeness of thought, and in consequence cannot consistently allow any motive to desire, but the image of a past pleasure or pain.[33]

At best, then, desires are suspended in favor of more pressing ones. In fact, the highest morality itself, presumably the most transcendent ground for suspension of desires, is based on this principle, as Locke suggests in Article 72 of the *Essay*. Speaking of "morality, established on its true foundations," Locke argues: "The rewards and punishments of the afterlife, which the Almighty has established as the enforcement of His law, are weight enough to determine the choice . . ." [34] when they are taken into account (which, apparently, they all too seldom are). Thus, the rewards and punishments of the afterlife are simply additions to a series of pleasures and pains the absence or presence of which, actual or anticipated on the basis of past experience, produces "uneasiness." Indeed, there seems to be no reason to regard Locke's power to suspend the satisfaction of immediate desires as anything very different from Hobbes' *prudence*, which is never regarded as incompatible with his mechanistic conception of man and human liberty.

It may perhaps be pointed out that, despite the suggested similarities between Hobbes and Locke on this point, it is precisely and explicitly Hobbes' moral doctrine that Locke is attacking in the *Essay*. And yet it can be argued that the very nature of Locke's attack on Hobbes is such that, far from revealing a truly fundamental difference between the two thinkers, it serves only to emphasize the fundamental similarities between their respective conceptions of man and human freedom.

The only mention of Hobbes in the *Essay* appears in Locke's account of moral obligation and the differing opinions men have concerning its foundation. Locke contrasts the Hobbesian

33 Thomas Hill Green, *Hume and Locke*, intro. Ramon M. Lamos (New York: Thomas Y. Crowell Co., 1968), pp. 315–317.
34 Locke, *Essay*, p. 364 (art. 72).

notion of obligation (or rather Locke's own interpretation of that notion) with "the true ground of morality." The Hobbesian principle is that men must obey certain moral laws "because the public requires it, and the Leviathan will punish you if you do not." [35] The "true ground of morality," on the other hand, "can only be the will and law of a God, who sees men in the dark, has in his hand rewards and punishments, and power enough to call to account the proudest offender." [36]

The disagreement, then, seems to be largely over who "has in his hands" the most impressive rewards and punishments, and not about the nature of human motivation or the relation between freedom and determination by external forces. The moral nature of man—which is the highest expression of whatever freedom he has—lies not so much in his ability, by virtue of his reason, to transcend determination by external stimuli, but simply in the source of the stimuli that act most strongly on him: a man's behavior is moral insofar as it is determined by rewards and punishments anticipated from God, as he is depicted in the Bible, rather than from some other source of rewards and punishments. Moral "action" is not qualitatively different from any other pleasure-pain-determined behavior. Again, at best, morality for Locke is a prudence very much like that of Hobbes' obedience to the sovereign. Locke's moral doctrine does not seem in the least incompatible with Hobbes' picturesquely mechanistic image of human behavior, according to which rewards and punishments are the "nerves" of the body politic which are "but so many strings . . . by which fastened to the seate of the Soveraignty every member is moved to perform his duty." [37]

The case of Mill is rather more complicated, primarily because there is an obvious, almost explicit, contradiction, of which Mill himself seems to have been aware, between his fa-

---

35 *Ibid.*, p. 69 (Bk I, chap. i, art. 5).
36 *Ibid.*, p. 70 (art. 6).
37 Thomas Hobbes, *Leviathan* (Oxford: Clarendon Press, 1909), Hobbes's Introduction, p. 8.

mous doctrine of liberty and individuality and his more general conception of man. The problem revolves essentially around Mill's conception of the self, which he shares with Hume and ultimately with Locke: the notion of the self as simply a series of sensations or possibilities of response. The difficulty is clearly that such a conception of the self cannot sustain a principle of individuality based on individual spontaneity, autonomy, and the primacy of the self. In general, Mill's defense of liberty and the uniqueness and spontaneity of individuality seems almost an aberration in the light of his other doctrines. Both before and after "On Liberty," for example, he adheres to a naturalistic conception of man, according to which human action becomes a reflex of independently existing natural forces: before "On Liberty," in his *Logic,* which argues for the possibility of a social science precisely on the grounds that social laws can be regarded as natural laws, and that the same laws of causality apply to men as to matter;[38] after, in the essays on religion, where we are told that "Art is as much Nature as anything else" in its causal determination.[39] As for *Utilitarianism,* the contradictions seem to exist side by side in a single work. Even if Mill's doctrine of liberty cannot be dismissed as an aberration, the fact remains that the kind of determinism implicit in his naturalism, in his concept of a social science, etc., is more compatible with his account of the knowing subject and the self as a series of sensations or possibilities of response, than it is with a conception of liberty that emphasizes the precedence of the self, the individual, the idea of self-development and spontaneity.[40]

The feeling that Mill's concept of liberty and individuality is a foreign element in his doctrine is strengthened by a com-

---

38 John Stuart Mill, *A System of Logic* (London: Longmans, Green and Co., 1967), p. 227 (Bk. III, chap. 5, art. 8, note) and Bk. VI *passim.*
39 Mill, *Three Essays on Religion,* quoted in R. Anschutz, *The Philosophy of J. S. Mill* (Oxford: Clarendon Press, 1953), p. 170.
40 It may be worth noting that the relationship between Mill's epistemology and that of Locke is far from indirect. As Anschutz points out, Mill acknowledges that he derived his basic epistemological principles from Hartley and Priestley, who, in turn, had adopted Locke's premises. See Anschutz, *op. cit.,* p. 174.

parison with the ideas of another advocate of individuality by whom Mill himself was greatly impressed. In "On Liberty," Mill singles out the doctrine of Wilhelm von Humboldt as a uniquely important statement of the philosophy of individual liberty that he himself is now propounding. The significant point is that, while for Mill that philosophy represents a departure from his other philosophical principles—notably his conception of mind and the self—Humboldt's doctrine of individuality is firmly and explicitly based on his own conception of mind and the self. What makes this consideration particularly important in the present argument is the fact that the theory of mind and self upon which Humboldt bases his doctrine of liberty is a fundamentally "Kantian" one. Particularly in his explanation of language, Humboldt develops a theory of mind according to which language is a creative phenomenon, the primary expression of the mind's creativity, generated out of principles of order supplied to experience a priori by the mind, the self-active subject. This conception of man's fundamental creativity becomes the basis of Humboldt's conception of freedom and individuality.[41]

The foregoing discussion should already give some indication of the bearing that the theories of mind here being examined may have on social and political thought. At this point it may be worth remembering the suggestion that not only can a theory

---

[41] It is significant too, that Humboldt develops a theory of sociality as a fact of human consciousness, dialectically united with individuality: "But since man is a social animal this being his distinctive character—because he needs others, not for protection, not for help, not for procreation, not for his life of habit (as do several animal species as well) but because he rises to a consciousness of self, and an 'I' without a 'thou' is an absurdity to his reason and his senses: therefore, in his own individuality (in his 'I'), the individuality of his society (his 'thou') defines itself simultaneously." Wilhelm von Humboldt, "Betrachtungen über die Weltgeschichte," *Gesammelte Schriften* (Berlin: Prussian Academy of Sciences, 1904) 3, 355: "Da aber der Mensch in Thier der Gesellligkeit ist—sein distinctiver Charakter—weil er eines Andern nicht zum Schutz, zur Hülfe, zur Zeugung, zum Gewohnheitsleben (wie einige Thierarten), sondern deshalb bedarf, weil er sich zum Bewusstseyn des Ichs erhebt, und ich ohne Du vor seinem Verstand und seiner Empfindung ein Undig sind; so reisst sich in seiner Individualität (in seinem Ich) zugleich die seiner Gessellschaft (seines Du) los."

of mind have such implications, but the theory may even in a sense have its origins in political philosophy, as seems to be the case with Kant. It is well known that Kant had the greatest admiration for Rousseau, by whom he was influenced despite the profound differences in their temperaments and their philosophical concerns and methods. Kant went so far as to suggest that Rousseau was the Newton of the moral sciences.[42] Generally, interpretations of Rousseau's influence on Kant refer to the respect for the moral nature of man and for the dignity of the common man which Kant learned from Rousseau and which, for example, lies at the heart of Kant's republicansim; or reference is made to the concept of freedom as obedience to self-imposed law, central both to Rousseau's political theory—for example, to his concept of the general will—and to Kant's moral philosophy and his concept of the rational will; or, related to this last point, similarities are seen between Rousseau's concept of the general will and Kant's categorical imperative. Moreover, in chapter 3 below, similarities between Kant and Rousseau's accounts of the beginnings of human history will be noted. In any event, the connections most commonly mentioned are specifically between Kant's moral and political philosophy and the moral and political thought of Rousseau. The object here, however, will be to suggest a more fundamental connection between Kant's philosophy in general, particularly his concept of mind, and the political philosophy of Rousseau.

Hegel himself, in fact, notes precisely such a fundamental connection in his argument that Rousseau, together with Hume, is the initiator of the transition to the new German philosophy. In Rousseau's political thought Hegel seems to find the principle of freedom that is essential to Kantian philosophy. Rousseau's theory of the state—presumably his concept of the general will, in particular—according to Hegel brings to consciousness

. . . the sense that man has liberty in his spirit as the altogether ab-

---

42 See Kant, *Fragmente*, in *Werke*, ed. E. Cassirer *et al.* (Berlin: Bruno Cassirer Verlag, 1912–1922), VIII, 630.

solute, that free-will is the notion of man. Freedom is just thought itself; he who casts thought aside and speaks of freedom knows not what he is talking of. The unity of thought with itself is freedom, the free will. Thought, as volition merely, is the impulse to abrogate one's subjectivity, the relation to present existence, the realizing of oneself, since in that I am endeavouring to place myself as existent on an equality with myself as thinking. It is only as having the power to think that the will is free. The principle of freedom emerged in Rousseau, and gave to man who apprehends himself as infinite, this infinite strength. This finishes the transition to the Kantian philosophy, which, theoretically considered, made this principle its foundation, knowledge aimed at freedom and at a content which it possesses in consciousness.[43]

Perhaps we can take the liberty of elaborating on Hegel's suggestion, with the possibility that it will be given a meaning somewhat different from what Hegel intended. Hegel seems to be suggesting that Rousseau's political theory is based on a conception of freedom as subjectivity, as self-activity in accordance with self-imposed law. Such a conception would be opposed to the determinism of empiricism, to the particular conceptions of liberty and free will that are implicit in it, and to the utilitarian concepts of the state, already exemplified by Hobbes and Locke, that can be associated with philosophical empiricism. For the empiricists, as we shall see, the self is essentially a reflection, a passive function of objective conditions, in the sense that it is nothing but a series of sensations or the awareness that accompanies each sensation, rather than a distinct, constant, positive "motif" of the mind, an "original activity," as it were. Activity takes the form of response to stimuli, the kind of self-passivity expressed by the pleasure-pain principle. As we have seen, volition tends to be thought of as simply reflexive, responsive motion, so that even action in accordance with individual will is nevertheless externally determined. Thus, freedom, which seems to mean simply the absence of external impediments to responsive motion, may still involve mechanistic determination and determination of the self by objects external to it.

43 Hegel, *op. cit.*, p. 402.

The same ideas are reflected in political theory. A theory of the state that is, for example, based on property, the concept of interest, and the interaction of interests reflects this kind of empiricist determinism, because it tends to identify man and his individuality with, to make him a function of, the external-ized, objectified conditions of his class, his place in society or the market, the division of labor, and so on.[44] Freedom in so-ciety, then, has to do with the free interplay of these objective forces and the proper functioning of the mechanism.

Rousseau, like Marx after him, seeks a principle of society that transcends this mechanistic determinism by basing his po-litical theory on the possibility of man's conscious and rational transcendence of objective forces. Firstly, by himself becoming the source of the public or general will, the source of the law, the individual is no longer subjected to a state separable from and against him. For empiricism-liberalism, the state must, in a sense, personify and objectify the law and the public interest and impose them from without upon egoistic individuals inter-acting in terms of their conflicting private interests. Because men are essentially "private" and egoistic, the people cannot serve as their own source of the general will. They must be repre-sented.[45] Secondly, the social revolution establishing a funda-mental equality, which is envisaged by Rousseau as a precondi-tion to his new political order, is meant to create a situation wherein man will no longer define his identity in terms of his objective status or function in the social system or the market. In effect, Rousseau's political society is based on autonomous, self-active individuals acting in accordance with self-imposed laws and a self-generated general will—in a sense, subjects which are themselves the sources of objectivity and universality.

Ernst Cassirer elaborates on this aspect of Rousseau's phi-losophy in connection with the latter's religious thought. The basis of natural religion, according to Rousseau, is man's ca-

---

44 For a more detailed discussion of these points, see below, pp. 152 ff.
45 For further explanation of this idea, see below, chap. 4, " 'Civil Society' and 'Human Society.' "

pacity to transcend by means of the rational will and self-imposed law the compulsion of external objects. The self is the source of religion, the voice of God, precisely insofar as it is capable of something more than receptivity, passivity, and response to stimulus. How Rousseau develops this idea in his religious doctrine is not important here. What is significant is the general principle the idea contains, the concept of the self it opposes to that of deterministic empiricism. As Cassirer points out:

> At this point Rousseau transcends the limitations of the sensationalistic psychology. The self is not a datum of sense and can never be understood as the mere product of sense data. It is an original activity, and the only evidence of such activity available to man. And this spontaneity of the self, not its receptivity, is the mark of the Divine.[46]

Thus, Rousseau's moral and political philosophy establishes the principle of freedom as autonomous self-activity, the principle of the self as originally creative and spontaneous rather than simply receptive, and the principle that the self, the subject, is the source of objectivity, generality, universality. Hegel's analysis, like that of Cassirer,[47] seems to suggest that Kant is attempting to find a systematic philosophical and epistemological basis for the concept of man and the self—the self as an "original activity" and the source of universality—that is implicit in Rousseau's moral and political thought.

46 Ernst Cassirer, *Rousseau, Kant and Goethe,* trans. J. Gutman, P. O. Kristeller, J. H. Randall, Jr.; introd. P. Gay (New York: Harper and Row Torchbooks, 1963), pp. 46–47.
47 See, for example, *ibid.,* p. 59.

2. The Psychological Dimension: Self and Other

> But since man is a social animal—this being his distinctive character—because he needs others, not for protection, not for help, not for procreation, not for his life of habit (as do several animal species as well), but because he rises to a consciousness of self, and an "I" without a "thou" is an absurdity to his reason and his senses; therefore, in his own individuality (in his "I,") the individuality of his society (his "thou"), defines itself simultaneously.[1]
>
> WILHELM VON HUMBOLDT
> *Observations on World History*

Consciousness and the Self

The foregoing brief outline of the Kantian theory of mind, and the way in which it lays the groundwork for a dialectical union of subject and object, can now be extended to a more specific consideration of that theory's implications for the idea of *self*, the relation between self and other, and the nature of individuality. The notion of the self is, of course, inextricably bound up with the problem of *consciousness*, since whatever else may be meant by that term, surely part of what it means to be *conscious* by any definition is to possess a *self*, to have some kind of awareness of one's "I" and its distinctness from "other." Needless to say, conceptions of the nature of consciousness—and hence, the nature of self-consciousness—will vary according to conceptions of the nature of mind. Moreover, insofar as the self is, as it were, the essence of subjectivity, clearly what is said abstractly about the epistemological relation between subject and object has concrete meaning in terms of psychological conceptions of the self and its relation to other—to objects, to its environment, to other selves.

[1] See above, p. 42 n. 41, for original text and citation.

Several important points which will emerge in the course of this discussion and in the subsequent chapters should be noted and emphasized at the outset. In the first chapter, it was suggested that in the Kantian view the subject is in a sense original and self-active, which would seem to imply that the self or the ego is, so to speak, a priori. Moreover, if this were the case, one might even be inclined to conclude that Kant is positing some kind of immutable "essence" of man that would entail a static conception of human nature. In fact, however, it turns out that the view that emphasizes the self-activity of the subject, in keeping with its dialectical approach, tends to encourage a more dynamic conception of human nature; and, again dialectically, it issues in a concept of the conscious self, not as a priori, but as an evolving phenomenon, something that must in a sense be *achieved*. The self in any meaningful sense is not simply the immediate, passive, perhaps even fleeting awareness accompanying individual sense impressions, which it seems to be for the empiricists. Instead, the *self* as a distinct and positive "theme" of the mind is the end product of the synthetic activity of mind. The conscious self is achieved through the dialectical interaction of the active mind and experience, of the perceiving subject and external objects. And as the product of a dialectical process, the self is a dynamic phenomenon, which, moreover, is in a very fundamental sense united with its other.

The empiricist's view, according to which the subject passively reflects or simply responds to objective reality, on the other hand, paradoxically seems to conceive of the self—as active ego or even egoism—as the primary and unchangeable fact of human existence. Since the self here seems to be little more than the simple awareness accompanying sense impressions, or at most a potential for response to objective reality, it may seem absurd to speak of the active ego as a priori. But this is perhaps one of the fundamental paradoxes of empiricist psychology. On the one hand, the self seems to have no distinct positive reality for the British empiricists; on the other hand, the same empiricists seem invariably to assume the existence of ego as a constant and active force. Given the empiricist's notion of the self as a kind of potential for responsive behavior, however, perhaps it can simply be said that this seemingly empty self takes on a positive content as egoism when that passivity is translated into activity in the form of *passion*. Passion is, so to speak, active passivity, responsive, reflexive action; and passion in a sense becomes the essence of the self.[2] Paradoxically, then, this passive almost non-existent selfhood becomes, in the form of passion, active egoism; and egoism becomes the primary and unchanging fact of human nature. We shall see that active egoism becomes in effect the immutable essence of man, the constant factor throughout every stage of human development. In fact, it should also become apparent that human *individuality* is virtually equated with egoism, a fact that has crucial implications for the nature of "Lockean" *individualism*.

To return, then, to an elaboration of these points, we may begin with a brief account of the empiricist conceptions of consciousness and the self and then contrast them with the Kantian conceptions.

Consciousness for Locke is apparently nothing more than the simple, irreducible, essentially passive awareness that is involved in all perception, "it being impossible for anyone to perceive without *perceiving* that he does perceive."[3] It is this "conscious-

2 The way in which passivity is translated into activity in the form of passion is best illustrated by the metaphor of matter in motion so popular in seventeenth- and eighteenth-century explanations of human behavior. Human passion, as responsive behavior, operates in much the same way as the physical phenomena of attraction and repulsion. Why passions should be assumed to be essentially egoistic—and even antagonistic—is not entirely clear, but perhaps the same metaphor, especially for example as used by Hobbes, provides a clue. The assumptions underlying the metaphor of matter in motion are atomistic, based on a model of separate and discrete particles whose relationships, such as they are, must ultimately take the form of collision.

3 John Locke, *An Essay Concerning Human Understanding*, ed. Alexander Campbell Fraser (New York: Dover Publications, 1959), I, 449 (Bk. II, chap. xxvii, art. 11). Hereafter referred to as *Essay*.

ness always accompanying thinking [here synonymous with perceiving. E. W.] . . . which makes everyone to be what he calls self, and thereby distinguishes himself from all other thinking things [and] in this alone consists personal identity. . . ." [4] Thus, consciousness of self is involved in any sense perception and represents no distinctive act of mind; in this sense, even an infant—perhaps even a child in the womb[5]—insofar as it can feel hunger and warmth, for example, has a consciousness of self. Locke, therefore, simply equates consciousness with sensation and feeling and the kind of awareness they imply.

It is not very far from this conception of the self as simply the "consciousness always accompanying thinking" or perceiving to Hume's explicit denial of any distinctive consciousness of self:

> But self or person is not any one impression, but that to which our several impressions and ideas are supposed to have a reference. If any impression gives rise to the idea of self, that impression must continue invariably the same, thro' the whole course of our lives; since self is suppos'd to exist after that manner. But there is no impression constant and invariable. Pain and pleasure, grief and joy, passions and sensations succeed each other, and never all exist at the same time. It cannot, therefore, be from any of these impressions, or from any other, that the idea of self is deriv'd; and consequently there is no such idea.[6]

Hume's doubts are shared by J. S. Mill, who finds himself unable to construct a more satisfactory conception of the self on the basis of the theory of mind he has inherited from Locke:

> The belief I entertain that my mind exists when it is not feeling, nor thinking, nor conscious of its own existence resolves itself into the belief of a Permanent Possibility of these states. . . . [Hence we may regard mind] as nothing but a series of our sensations (to which must

---

4 *Ibid.*

5 See *Ibid.*, p. 184 (Bk. II, chap. ix, art. 4), on the existence of ideas in the unborn child.

6 David Hume, *A Treatise of Human Nature*, ed. L. A. Selby-Bigge (Oxford: Clarendon Press, 1888), pp. 251–252 (Bk. I, chap. ix, sec. vi). Hereafter referred to as *Treatise*.

now be added our internal feelings) as they actually occur, with the addition of infinite possibilities of feeling requiring for their actual realization conditions which may or may not take place.[7]

In the face of such a conception of mind and self, Mill can only resign himself to the difficulty posed by the fact that we are also aware of ourselves *as* such a series of sensations:

> . . . we are reduced to the alternative of believing that the mind, or ego, is something different from any series of feelings or possibilities of them, or of accepting the paradox that something which *ex hypothesi* is but a series of feelings, can be aware of itself as series. . . . I think by far the wisest thing we can do is to accept the inexplicable fact, without any theory as to how it takes place; and when we are obliged to speak of it in terms which assume a theory, to use them with a reservation as to their meaning.[8]

It cannot be emphasized enough that the most serious difficulties encountered by Hume and Mill in their analyses of the self revolve around the very themes that are central to this essay. In Mill's case, as we have already seen, the empiricist conception of self endangers his conceptions of liberty and individuality. In Hume's case, which will be discussed more fully later, that conception of the self becomes the source of his gravest philosophical doubts precisely because it cannot support his conception of sympathy, the basis of community. To sustain their most cherished doctrines, both Hume and Mill feel the need for a more positive conception of the self than their theories of mind will allow. It is precisely this kind of conception of the self that Kant tries to develop on the basis of his new theory of mind.

In the previous chapter, the meaning of Kant's epistemology and of his opposition to classical empiricism was illustrated by a discussion of his distinction between perception and experience. From his conception of that distinction, it should be clear

---

[7] John Stuart Mill, *Examination of Sir William Hamilton's Philosophy*, quoted in R. Anschutz, *The Philosophy of J. S. Mill* (Oxford: Clarendon Press, 1953), p. 179.
[8] *Ibid.*

that Kant differentiates between the kind of awareness implicit in perception and a distinctive, more active, in a sense independent, form of consciousness corresponding to experience. By the same token, there is a difference between the "self" that simply "accompanies" each perception, and the distinct, positive, and continuous experience of the self involved in true self-consciousness:

> This thoroughgoing identity of the apperception of a manifold which is given in intuition contains a synthesis of representations, and is possible only through the consciousness of this synthesis. For the empirical consciousness, which accompanies different representations, is in itself diverse and without relation to the identity of the subject. That relation comes about, not simply through my accompanying each representation with consciousness, but only in so far as I conjoin one representation with another, and am conscious of the synthesis of them. Only in so far, therefore, as I can unite a manifold of given representations in *one consciousness,* is it possible for me to represent to myself the *identity of the consciousness* in (i.e. throughout) *these representations.* . . .
>
> . . . In other words, only in so far as I can grasp the manifold of the representations in one consciousness, do I call them one and all *mine.* For otherwise I should have as many-coloured and diverse a self as I have representations of which I am conscious to myself.[9]

Moreover, just as the relationship between perception and experience is developmental in the growth of the individual psyche, so the consciousness of self is the product of that evolution from perception to the capacity for experience, an evolution that Kant regards as the child's "development into humanity" *(Entwicklung zur Menschheit).*[10] In the period of "scattered perceptions" prior to the "time of experience," the child "merely *felt* itself; now it thinks itself." [11] And, again, as might be concluded from our discussion of the evolution from percep-

---

9 Immanuel Kant, *Critique of Pure Reason,* trans. Norman Kemp Smith (New York: St. Martin's Press, 1965), pp. 153–154.
10 Kant, *Anthropologie in pragmatischer Hinsicht,* in *Gesammelte Schriften* (Berlin: Prussian Academy of Sciences, 1917), VII, 128.
11 *Ibid.,* p. 127: "Vorher fühlte es bloss sich selbst, jetzt denkt es sich selbst."

tion to experience, the attainment of selfhood, the progress from the self as simply the awareness accompanying all perception to the self as true self-consciousness, is accomplished through a process of confrontation with the external world. In other words, the consciousness of self is not simply given but must, in a sense, be achieved. An infant can *feel*, but it is not yet conscious of itself in the complex, active sense implied by its later use of the pronoun "I." The active, conscious, and progressive process of delimiting subjectivity from objectivity, "I" from "not-I," has not yet taken place, since there is only direct, simple awareness of sensation and feeling unmediated by true consciousness. The 'I' is not yet an object for consciousness. The final, distinctly conscious "I" is a product of various processes of delineation, requiring a variety of confrontations with "otherness" for the mind to work with.

In short, Kant, unlike Locke, distinguishes among the various levels of "selfhood," particularly between, on the one hand, the simple basic, immediate, and essentially passive and unconscious "self" which is involved in sensation and, of course, underlies all experience; and on the other hand, the truly conscious self which is the end, rather than the beginning, of a mental process, the self that becomes possible only when the "I" can become an object for consciousness. The original sensate "self"—if it can, in fact, be isolated and identified—is, of course, necessary to make experience possible; but the true, conscious self is a result of experience, a product of differentiation and combination. The constitution of the self in the latter sense involves a *synthesis* of the discrete and passive sensations of the rudimentary "self" into a unity; and it is precisely the consciousness of this power of combination, this "act of spontaneity," that produces man's experience of himself as intelligence, as a free and spontaneous being—an experience that, as we have seen, is so central to Kant's doctrine of freedom. Moreover, the process is one that arises out of a dialectical union of self and other, both in the sense that it is a product of the interaction of subject and object, the activity of mind and external objects, and in the sense that the self can arise only out of a prior unity with its environment, objects and other selves. The "I" defines itself only through relationships with its "other," particularly its "thou."

The Neo-Kantian Ernst Cassirer elaborates these points in such a way as to make them even more strikingly pertinent to the present discussion. In the *Philosophy of Symbolic Forms,* Cassirer suggests that this inseparability of subject and object, self and other, has its social counterpart in the inseparability of individual and community. The mythical form of consciousness that characterizes primitive man at first unites the self with the community and only progressively makes way for individuation. In this sense, as in others that will be discussed in the course of this study, the "Kantian" approach dialectically unites individuality and community:

> The opposition of subject and object, the differentiation of the I from all given, determinate things, is not the only form in which progress is made from a general, still undifferentiated life feeling to the consciousness of the self. In the sphere of pure knowledge, it is true, progress consists above all in the differentiation of the principle of knowledge from its content, of the knower from the known; but mythical consciousness and religious feeling embrace a still more fundamental contrast. Here the I is oriented not immediately toward the outside world but rather toward a personal existence and life similar to it in kind. Subjectivity has as its correlate not some outward thing but rather a "thou" or "he," *from which on the one hand it distinguishes itself, but with which on the other hand it groups itself.* This thou or he forms the true antithesis which the I requires in order to find and define itself. For here again the individual feeling and consciousness of self stand not at the beginning but at the end of the process of development. In the earliest stages to which we can trace back this development we find the feeling of *self* immediately fused with a definite mythical-religious feeling of *community.* The I feels and knows itself only insofar as it takes itself as a member of a community, insofar as it sees itself grouped with others into the unity of a family, a tribe, a social organism. Only in and through this social organism does it possess itself; every manifestation of its own personal existence and life is

linked, as though by invisible magic ties, with the life of the totality around it.[12]

Individuality and the Ego   .

Up to now, our discussion has dealt more with the problem of *freedom* than with *community*. Needless to say, the relation between self and other is significant for the problem of community largely insofar as "other" means not only inanimate "objective" reality or external *things* but, above all, other *men*. Here, the relevance of the previously discussed subject-object problem rests largely on the degree to which other men must be regarded as the partners in the dialectical unity required for the process of individuation and the development of ego—the degree to which, in other words, community must be regarded as the condition for individuality, and vice versa. The passage from Cassirer cited above indicates how the subject-object relationship finds its social reflection in an individual-community relationship, and how the relationship between individuality and community is reciprocal. The implication of this dialectical view is that individualism is not synonymous with egoism. Far from seeing egoistic individualism as the natural, even logical, consequence of man's unique capacity to be conscious of himself, this view regards self-consciousness and ego as both derived from and conducive to sociality.

One aspect of this argument that is particularly worthy of elaboration concerns the implications of the chronology of self-consciousness and ego-development suggested by Kantian psychology. The importance of the argument that consciousness of self is not primary is obvious enough in its implications for the relationship between the individual and other men. The argument becomes even more significant when transposed from the history of individual consciousness to the history of mankind and the transition from nature to culture. All forms of the argu-

12 Ernst Cassirer, *The Philosophy of Symbolic Forms* (New Haven: Yale University Press, 1953), Vol. II, "Myth," p. 175. Emphasis added.

ment appear in Kant, who discusses the derivative nature of self-consciousness in his *Critique of Pure Reason*, the lateness of the child's ego-consciousness in his *Anthropology*, and the transition from an undifferentiated preconscious "life feeling" to a self-aware social consciousness in his "Conjectural Beginning of Human History." Unfortunately, however, Kant himself never elaborates the implications of these views in any great detail; nor do his immediate successors concern themselves specifically with such psychological questions as the process of ego development and individuation. Nevertheless, we may perhaps allow ourselves the liberty of, in a sense, reconstructing a "Kantian" theory of child psychology by examining the view of a psychologist whose assumptions are strikingly Kantian, not only with respect to the specific problem of individuality, but even with respect to the underlying theory of mind. A most detailed and explicit illustration of the implications that certain Kantian principles may have for these questions is provided by a modern psychologist, Jean Piaget. To justify the use of his example, however, a few words must be said first about Piaget's theory of mind and the sense in which it might be called Kantian.[13] It may be that Piaget's formulation will even serve to clarify to some extent Kant's own theory of mind.

To begin with, Piaget, like Kant, opposes his theory to traditional empiricism and its modern heirs; and he does so not because of the importance empiricism attaches to experience, but on the grounds that it assigns a purely passive, receptive role to the subject in experience. Here is how Piaget describes the doctrine he opposes:

> . . . In short, at every level, experience is necessary to the development of intelligence. That is the fundamental fact on which empirical hypotheses are based and which they have the merit of calling

13 Piaget himself acknowledges the affinities between his theory of mind and that of Kant. See, for example, his *The Origin of Intelligence in Children*, trans. Margaret Cook (New York; W. W. Norton and Co., 1963), pp. 376 ff. It must be said, however, that Piaget does not seem to give Kant his due. As the subsequent quotations from Piaget will show, the affinities are more profound than he admits.

to attention. On this question our analyses of the origin of the child's intelligence confirm that point of view. But there is more to empiricism than just an affirmation of the role of experience: Empiricism is primarily a certain conception of experience and its action. On the one hand, it tends to consider experience as imposing itself without the subject's having to organize it, that is to say, as impressing itself directly on the organism without activity of the subject being necessary to constitute it. On the other hand, and as a result, empiricism regards experience as existing by itself and either owing its value to a system of external ready-made "things" and of given relations between those things (metaphysical empiricism) or consisting in a system of self-sufficient habits and associations (phenomenalism). This dual belief in the existence of an experience in itself and in its direct pressure on the subject's mind explains, in the last analysis, why empiricism is necessarily associationist. Every method of recording experience other than association in its different forms (conditioned reflex, "associative transfer," association of images, etc.) presupposes an intellectual activity partaking of the construction of the external reality perceived by the subject.[14]

To this view according to which the subject is simply receptive and the object is something that is given rather than constituted by the subject, Piaget opposes a conception of the active subject that, so to speak, participates in the creation of the object—that is, objectifies experience by means of the synthetic activity of mind. It will be recalled that this notion that the *object* is not simply given but is rather the end product of mental synthesis plays an essential role in the Kantian idea of *self*. It will be seen that this notion plays a similarly crucial role in Piaget's account of the process of individuation, the differentiation of "I" from "not-I." Like Kant, Piaget clearly distinguishes between simple sensation and a higher level of consciousness in which, through a process of mental synthesis, experience is "objectified," or, to put it another way, the self and objects of experience are differentiated from each other:

The mind, then, proceeds from pure phenomenalism whose representations remain half-way between the body and the external en-

14 *Ibid.*, p. 362.

vironment, to active experimentation which alone penetrates inside things. What does this mean, if not that the child does not undergo simple external pressure from the environment but tries, on the contrary, to adapt himself to it? Experience, accordingly, is not reception but progressive action and construction: That is the fundamental fact. . . . Now this first reason for correcting the empirical interpretation entails a second one. If the "object" is not imposed at the beginning of mental evolution but is proposed as highest goal, would this not be because it cannot be conceived independently of an activity of the subject? . . . It is, in effect, to the extent that the subject is active that experience is objectified. Objectivity does not therefore mean independence in relation to the assimilatory activity of intelligence, but simply dissociation from the self and from egocentric subjectivity. The objectivity of experience is an achievement of accommodation and assimilation combined, that is to say, of the intellectual activity of the subject, and not a primary datum imposed on him from without.[15]

Thus, subject and object are united, both in the sense that objectivity is a function of the subject, of mental activity, and in the sense that what might be called *conscious* subjectivity, selfhood, is a product of this process of objectification, the differentiation of self and other from a prior undifferentiated unity. We can now go on to see how Piaget elaborates this dialectical relationship between subject and object into a more explicit theory of ego development, how individuality and sociality, like subjectivity and objectivity, dialectically interact.

The crucial point in Piaget's account of ego development in the child is that it seeks to demonstrate the "solidarity between the social and the individual. . . ." [16] Moreover, interestingly enough, "the most fundamental example of this solidarity . . . is that of the consciousness of self." [17] That the consciousness of

15 *Ibid.*, pp. 365–367.
16 Jean Piaget, *The Moral Judgment of the Child*, trans. M. Gabain (New York: Collier Books, 1962), p. 387. Part of this analysis is drawn from Piaget's discussion of J. M. Baldwin, with particular reference to the latter's *Psychology and Sociology*; but Piaget makes it quite clear that, as far as this aspect of the question is concerned, he shares Baldwin's view.
17 *Ibid.*

self should serve as an example of the solidarity between the social and the individual is, of course, striking exactly because, as Piaget himself points out, "What could be more intimate and more strictly 'individual' in appearance than the feeling of being oneself and different from others?" [18]

The solidarity between the social and the individual is two-fold—or rather, reciprocal. First, the consciousness of self is a relatively late product of relations with others. This is an idea we have already encountered. Second, the achievement of a consciousness of self in turn provides the basis for social cooperation. Again, this interpretation of ego-consciousness is a clear example of a view that regards ego as a *basis* of sociality rather than its enemy.

In his discussion of J. M. Baldwin's analysis of consciousness of self, Piaget writes that this consciousness,

. . . is really the result of inter-individual actions and of imitation in particular. Far from starting from any consciousness of self, the baby is ignorant of himself as subject and locates his subjective states on the same plane as physical images: this is the "projective" stage. How then does the child ever come to discover himself? As far as his own body is concerned it is easy enough to see that he does so thanks to a progressive comparison of it with other bodies, a process which is part and parcel of learning to imitate. It is because it has a visual perception of another person's mouth and imitates the movements of this mouth that the baby of ten to twelve months learns to give its various buccal sensations an analogous form; and so on. In the same way with regard to psychical qualities, it is by imitating other people's behavior that the child will discover his own. In this way, the individual passes to the "subjective" stage in which he is conscious of possessing an "I" that is identical with others.[19]

Thus, a child becomes conscious of itself, develops an ego, through a process of comparison made possible by interpersonal relationships. The ego, then, is, with regard to its origin, a social phenomenon. Piaget, however, does not stop here. He goes on

18 *Ibid.*
19 *Ibid.*

in the same passage to demonstrate how the solidarity between social and individual operates in the opposite direction as well, how the consciousness of self in turn enhances, or even makes possible, cooperation and true sociality:

> . . . But once his attention has been directed upon himself in this way, the child becomes capable of the converse process. Having little by little come to assign to himself all the forms of conduct he has observed in others, he learns simultaneously to ascribe to others the feelings and motives of which he is conscious in himself. In this way there is constituted an "ejective" process which in its alterations with the other two (projective and subjective) constitute the whole of personal life. For as the shuttle flies backward and forward between ejection and imitation, equilibrium is maintained between consciousness of self and awareness of others, just as their mutual elaboration had been previously ensured by the same process.[20]

The contribution of the social to the individual has been reciprocated. The process of comparison whereby the child was able to differentiate himself from those around him is now the means by which he reunites himself with them through a perception of similarities which permit the growth of fellow-feeling. Moreover, there is a kind of inner necessity or logic to this process which makes the development of fellow-feeling and cooperation inevitable in normal development. Piaget summarizes his position this way:

> In order to discover oneself as a particular individual, what is needed is a continuous comparison, the outcome of opposition, of discussion, and of mutual control: and indeed consciousness of the individual self appears far later than consciousness of the more general features in our psychological make-up. *This is why a child can remain egocentric for a very long time (through lack of consciousness of self)*, while participating on all points in the minds of others. It is only by knowing our individual nature with its limitations as well as its resources that we grow capable of coming out of ourselves and collaborating with other individual natures. Consciousness of self is therefore both a product and a condition of cooperation.[21]

20 *Ibid.*, p. 388.
21 *Ibid.*, pp. 393–394 (emphasis added).

From the point of view of this discussion and particularly the effort to outline a conception of individualism that contrasts with the empirical-liberal conception, the most significant consequence of Piaget's analysis is that it quite deliberately and explicitly avoids equating ego and individuality with egoism or egocentrism. On the contrary, as the last quotation in particular indicates, egocentrism is the result of a *lack* of ego-consciousness, while the presence of such consciousness results in sociality. Piaget elaborates on this connection between egocentrism and the lack of ego-consciousness in his discussion of the child's initial inability to distinguish between external and internal, subjective and objective. This inability is a reflection of the absence of consciousness of self and would therefore seem, perhaps, to represent the diametrical opposite of egocentrism:

> Only—and this is the other side of the picture—as the child does not dissociate his ego from the environment, whether physical or social, he mixes into all his thoughts and all his actions ideas and practices that are due to the intervention of his ego and which, just because he fails to recognize them as subjective, exercise a check on his complete socialization. . . .
>
> . . . Egocentrism in so far as it means confusion of the ego and the external world, and egocentrism in so far as it means lack of cooperation constitute one and the same phenomenon.[22]

In short, egocentrism is ego-confusion or lack of ego, while ego-consciousness implies cooperation and sociality; it is not the ego that hinders socialization and cooperation, but the absence of ego. Surely nothing could be clearer than the contrast between this view and the empiricist-liberal view of ego and individualism. In the first place, it is rather unlikely that either Hobbes or Locke, for example, ever think in terms of a state of existence in which man is not conscious of himself, his ego. Their tendency always seems to be to take for granted the existence of ego and to assume the "I" as the ultimate, universal, and stable fact of human existence; and this applies as well to their treatments of

22 *Ibid.*, pp. 92–93.

the passage from the state of nature to civil society, which will be discussed later. Moreover, we have already noted how naturally that primary consciousness of self is associated with egoism, and the impression left by Locke's *Essay* is confirmed, for example, in his treatment of child psychology in *Some Thoughts Concerning Education*:

> I told you before, that children love liberty . . . I now tell you, they love something more; and that is dominion: and this is the first original of most vicious habits, that are ordinary and natural. This love of power and dominion shows itself very early, and that in these two things. We see children (as soon almost as they are born, I am sure long before they can speak) cry, grow peevish, sullen and out of humour, for nothing but to have their desires submitted to by others; they contend for a ready compliance from all about them, especially those that stand near or beneath them in age or degree, as soon as they come to consider others with those distinctions.
>
> Another thing, wherein they show their love of dominion, is their desire to have things to be theirs; they would have property and possessions, pleasing themselves with the power which that seems to give, and the right they thereby have to dispose of them as they please.[23]

Leaving aside for the moment the particular significance of the natural passions that Locke attributes to the child—love of power and possessions—the very language of the passage is revealing. It suggests that Locke is assuming the existence in the infant of an ego-consciousness and its associated egoism, which are essentially the same as the conscious egoism involved in adult possessiveness. Piaget, on the other hand, might interpret infant possessiveness as evidence of the child's inability to distinguish his ego from his surroundings.

At any rate, it would not be unfair to say that the very premise of empiricist-liberal individualism, as anticipated by Hobbes and reflected, in diluted form, by his liberal successors, is that ego is by very definition antisocial. To these thinkers, Piaget's

[23] Locke, *Some Thoughts Concerning Education*, in *The Works*, 12th ed. (London: C. & J. Rivington, 1824), VIII, 93–94 (art. 103–105).

suggestion that ego and egocentrism are incompatible and that individuality and sociality are ultimately one and the same would be logically and practically absurd.[24]

To summarize Piaget's position, then: Consciousness of self develops from an initially undifferentiated but "egocentric" oneness with all reality. The means whereby individuation takes place is a process of imitation and comparison made possible by relations with others. But once consciousness of self is achieved, the same process of comparison permits the perception of similarities between self and others, and through a process of "ejection," fellow-feeling and cooperation are actuated. Thus, ego is both a consequence of social relationships and the basis of sociality; and in this sense, the process of ejection is the foundation of social morality.

At this point it is impossible to avoid noting the striking similarities between Piaget's formulation of the moral development of children and Rousseau's in *Emile.* An account of Rousseau's ideas in this connection may be even more relevant to the question at hand, because Kant himself acknowledged Rousseau as his predecessor in many ways, and because Rousseau's social thought is in a very fundamental sense a direct and deliberate attack on the social doctrines of both Hobbes and Locke. Rousseau will also provide a convenient transition to the nature-culture problem, since his treatment of the latter neatly parallels his account of child development.

After describing the earliest stage of development in children, Rousseau continues:

With their strength develops the understanding which puts them in a position to direct it. It is at this second stage that individual life truly begins: it is then that the child becomes conscious of himself.[25]

24 For a discussion of an opposing view of Locke, see below pp. 89–96.
25 Jean-Jacques Rousseau, *Emile,* in *Œuvres Complètes* (Paris: Editions Gallimard, Bibliothèque de la Pléiade, 1969), IV, 301 (Bk. II): "Avec leur force se developpe la connoissance qui les met en état de la diriger. C'est à ce second degré que commence proprement la vie de l'individu, c'est alors qu'il prend la conscience de lui-même."

The child's first and most natural sentiment is self-love *(amour de soi)*,[26] but love of others naturally derives from it in the course of interpersonal relations: "The child's first sentiment is love of self, and the second, which derives from the first, is love of those near him. . . ."[27] The central concept of Rousseau's analysis is *compassion (pitié)*, "the first relative sentiment which touches the human heart according to the order of na-

---

It is also interesting to compare the following statement by Rousseau on the development of self-consciousness with Locke's observation about the infant's "love of power and dominion" cited above: "It is only by movement that we learn that there are things which are not the self, and it is only by our own movement that we acquire the idea of extension. It is because the child has no such idea that he stretches out his hand to seize an object whether it touches him or is a hundred paces away from him. This effort may seem to you to be a sign of tyranny, an order which he gives to the object to come to him or to you to bring it to him, but not at all; it is only that the same objects which he sees first in his brain, then before his eyes, he now sees at the tip of his fingers, and he cannot imagine any extension which is not within his reach." *Ibid.*, pp. 284–285: "Ce n'est que par le mouvement que nous apprenons qu'il ya a des choses qui ne sont pas nous, et ce n'est que par notre propre mouvement que nous aquérons l'idée de l'étendü. C'est parce que l'enfant n'a point cette idée qu'il tend indifféremment la main pour saisir l'objet qui le touche ou l'objet qui est à cent pas de lui. Cet effort qu'il fait vous paroit un signe d'empire, un ordre qu'il donne à l'objet de s'approcher ou à vous de la lui apporter, et point du tout; c'est seulement que les mêmes objets qu'il voyoit d'abord dans son cerveau, puis sur ses yeux, il les voit maintenant au bout de ses bras et n'imagine d'étendüe que celle ou il peut atteindre."
[26] Rousseau distinguishes between "amour de soi" (love of self) and "amour-propre" (vanity). For example: "Self-love, which concerns only ourselves, is content when our true needs are satisfied; but vanity, which compares self with others, is never content and cannot be, because this sentiment, while preferring ourselves to others, also demands that others prefer us to themselves, which is impossible. Thus, the gentle and warm passions arise from self-love, while the hateful and angry passions arise from vanity." *Ibid.*, p. 493: "L'amour de soi, qui ne regarde qu'à nous, est content quand nos vrais besoins sont satisfaits; mais l'amour-propre, qui se compare, n'est jamais content et ne sauroit l'être, parce que ce sentiment, en nous préférant aux autres, éxige aussi que les autres nous préférent à eux, ce qui est impossible. Voilà comment les passions douces et affectueuses naissent de l'amour de soi, et comment les passions haineuses et irascibles naissent de l'amour-propre."
[27] *Ibid.*, p. 492: "Le prémier sentiment d'un enfant est de s'aimer lui-même, et le second qui dérive du prémier est d'aimer ceux qui l'approchent. . . ."

ture." [28] Here is how Rousseau describes the growth of compassion:

> To become sensitive and compassionate a child must know that there are beings like himself who suffer what he has suffered, who feel the pains he has felt, and others of which he must have an idea, being able to feel them himself. Indeed how can we be moved by compassion, if not by taking ourselves outside ourselves, identifying ourselves with the suffering animal, leaving, so to speak, our own being to take on his? We suffer only insofar as we judge that he suffers; it is not in ourselves but in him that we suffer. Thus, one becomes sensitive only when his imagination is aroused and begins to take him outside himself.[29]

The point, however, is that here too there is a kind of internal necessity or psychic "logic" to this process—a process of "ejection"—that culminates in compassion. The "imagination" is naturally and inevitably aroused by the mere fact that the child has relationships with others and is endowed with reason which unavoidably compares and sees similarities. Compassion is a rather unique sentiment in that it depends on an act of reason, but an act of reason that is inseparable from a consequent sentiment. Thus, the feeling for others is the natural consequence of love of self, and that fellow-feeling is corrupted only by subsequent corrupt and "unnatural" social relations. In short, ego, the consciousness of which is necessary for self-love, is the basis of sociality and love of others; and social morality ultimately rests on the growth of compassion through a natural process of "ejection."

---

28 *Ibid.*, p. 505: "Ainsi nait la pitié, prémier sentiment relatif qui touche le coeur humain selon l'ordre de la nature."

29 *Ibid.*, pp. 505–506: "Pour devenir sensible et pitoyable, il faut que l'enfant sache qu'il y a des êtres semblables à lui qui souffrent ce qu'il a souffert, qui sentent les douleurs qu'il a senties, et d'autres dont il doit avoir l'idée, comme pouvant les sentir aussi. En effet, comment nous laissons-nous émouvoir à la pitié, si ce n'est en nous transportant hors de nous et nous identifiant avec l'animal souffrant, en quittant, pour ainsi dire, notre être pour prendre le sien: ce n'est pas dans nous, c'est dans lui que nous souffrons. Ainsi nul ne devient sensible que quand son imagination s'anime et commence à le transporter hors de lui."

This concept of compassion can, in fact, be regarded as the key to Rousseau's social thought, and it will appear again in our discussion of his anthropology. From the point of view of the "Kantian" approach, perhaps the most significant aspect of this concept of compassion—and Piaget's process of ejection—is their intellectual component or, rather, their union of the intellectual and the emotional. Just as the ejective process that gives birth to fellow-feeling is essentially an intellectual process based on the achievement of the consciousness of self, compassion is a feeling inescapably grounded in an act of consciousness and involves the ability to unite in consciousness the other with the newfound self. Compassion is possibly, as Lévi-Strauss argues in his discussion of Rousseau, ". . . the only psychic state of which the content is indissociably both affective and intellectual, and which the act of consciousness suffices to transfer from one level to the other."[30]

Again, as the subsequent discussion of the nature-culture transition will demonstrate more clearly, the union of intellectual and affective contained in the notion of compassion is twofold. The achievement of consciousness and the intellectual ability to differentiate implied by consciousness of self are dependent on a prior undifferentiated and "unconscious" feeling of unity with all reality and community with all life. But the intellectual ability to differentiate is itself the condition for a new feeling of community at a conscious level—the community with other differentiated selves. The act of individuation that creates the self is at the same time an act of unification with other individuals. Compassion is, then, a kind of synthesis of the early unconscious feeling of unity with the new consciousness of self, a synthesis that is expressed as a conscious feeling of community with other men.

It is illuminating to compare Rousseau's concept of compassion with Hume's idea of *sympathy,* especially since Hume is

[30] Claude Lévi-Strauss, *Totemism* trans. R. Needham (Boston: Beacon Press, 1963), p. 101.

generally classed among the empiricists and is often regarded as the bridge to Kantian philosophy. What is striking about Hume's idea is its similarity to Rousseau's. Since the usual tendency is to classify Hume with Locke, this similarity to Rousseau on a fundamental issue must be accounted for if we are to assume a significant degree of consistency in each thinker's philosophical orientation.[31]

The idea of sympathy plays a central role in Hume's conception of man:

No quality of human nature is more remarkable both in itself and

[31] The following account of Hume's idea of sympathy is based largely on the *Treatise of Human Nature.* A certain degree of controversy exists concerning the fate of that idea in Hume's later works, notably the *Enquiry Concerning the Principles of Morals.* L. A. Selby-Bigge in his introduction to the *Enquiry* (Oxford: Clarendon Press, 1902) and N. Kemp-Smith in *The Philosophy of David Hume* (London: Macmillan, 1949) suggest that, while sympathy still plays a central role in the *Enquiry,* there is no longer any attempt to explain its origin in the consciousness of self. Instead, Hume now contents himself with arguing that sympathy, which here simply stands for social sentiments such as humanity, benevolence, fellow-feeling, must be accepted as an ultimate. (See Kemp-Smith, pp. 151-152, and Selby-Bigge, p. xxvi.) John B. Stewart, in *The Moral and Political Philosophy of David Hume* (New York: Columbia University Press, 1963), argues at length that no recantation of Hume's earlier explanations of sympathy, either explicit or implicit, occurs in the *Enquiry* (pp. 331-339).

While the idea of the origin of sympathy in self-consciousness is central to our comparison of Hume and Rousseau, the controversy does not pose an insurmountable difficulty for the present argument. On the contrary, it perhaps strengthens the case being made here. Charles Hendel's interpretation, in *Studies in the Philosophy of David Hume* (Indianapolis: Bobbs-Merrill Co., 1963), seems to provide, at least implicitly, a way of reconciling the two views outlined above. As we shall see, Hendel suggests that Hume recognizes, in the Appendix to the *Treatise,* that his philosophical system, his theory of mind, cannot provide for the kind of positive consciousness of self that must be assumed to explain sympathy as a function of self-consciousness. This recognition would, of course, explain why in his later work Hume no longer tries to explain the origin of sympathy; but this does not mean that he has rejected his earlier explanation. On the contrary, Hume almost seems more prepared to abandon his philosophical system than to reject his explanation of sympathy. His inability to explain self-consciousness in terms of that system is one of the primary factors that compelled him to be far less ambitious in his later works and apparently to abandon his attempt to construct a "grand system" to replace Locke's, and that confirmed and deepened his philosophical skepticism.

in its consequences, than that propensity we have to sympathize with others, and to receive by communication their inclinations and sentiments, however different from or even contrary to our own.[32]

To the effects of sympathy, Hume attributes, for example, the similarities, often associated with race or national character, to be found among men of the same country. Above all, he derives from sympathy many of man's most essential passions, most particularly those contributing to sociality. Sympathy is the source of all social virtues; it is, indeed, the basis of human sociality. In fact, Hume seems ultimately to conclude that sympathy, its attendant social passions, and its compulsion toward a common life outweigh selfish egoism in human motivation.

This propensity to sympathize with other men depends, of course, on relations of "resemblance and contiguity" and man's ability to form an idea of similarities between his own experiences and those of others. As Charles Hendel in his study of Hume points out, however, Hume, unlike many other thinkers who have formulated ideas of human sympathy, is aware that the ability to form ideas of similarity or merely to recognize a feeling in another man is not in itself sufficient to account for the *feelings* aroused in oneself by sympathy. As Hendel puts it:

> But all these relations of resemblance, contiguity and causation would not make the mere idea of some impulse or feeling become the very feeling and activity itself. They might, indeed, produce a strong conviction in us of the reality of this tendency in the other person. We should certainly take it to be the fact, when we observe his expressions, that he actually feels this or that emotion. Yet, what happens is not simply a belief, but our own feelings of this particular sentiment. This must be due to a hidden factor that has not yet come into view.[33]

In effect, then, what Hume is trying to do—to return to our earlier discussion of Rousseau—is account for the unique unity of the "intellectual" and the "affective" in the phenomenon of

32 Hume, *Treatise*, p. 316.
33 Hendel, *op. cit.*, p. 230.

sympathy. A man's ability to compare what he sees in others to a particular experience of his own can account only for the formation in him of a *belief*—i.e., an intellectual phenomenon—concerning the others' feelings. Something else must account for the translation of that feeling into a feeling of his own. Although Hendel, despite his interest in Rousseau, fails to mention the similarity, Hume finds his solution in the same "hidden factor" that Rousseau uses to explain compassion. In short, Hume, like Rousseau, discovers, to use Hendel's phrase, that "sympathy is . . . a phase of our own self-consciousness." [34] A simple comparison of what we see in others to a given experience of our own can arouse feeling in us only insofar as that experience is ultimately associated with a deeper, distinct, and constant self-consciousness or "concern" with ourselves—what Hendel calls the self as an "activity or impulse," a "distinct motif of mind," [35] rather than the self simply as the irreducible awareness accompanying fleeting sense impressions. An impression received under the influence of that "impulse" has conferred upon it some of the strong "interest" associated with self-concern. In other words, by a process of "ejection," concern for self is extended to include concern for others, and their feelings become our own.

It is extremely important to note that in deriving sympathy from self-consciousness, Hume is *not* accepting the theory that social sentiments are simply the products of selfish egoism and self-interest mediated by prudence and utility. This theory was undoubtedly a popular one. It seems, for example, to be the basis of Bernard Mandeville's formula, "Private vices, publick benefits"; Alexander Pope's couplet in the "Essay on Man": "Thus God and Nature link'd the general frame, And bade Self-love and Social be the same"; Adam Smith's theory of the market; and even John Locke's political theory. Hume, how-

[34] *Ibid.*, p. 234.
[35] *Ibid.*, p. 231.

ever, was profoundly critical of this view. In his essay "Of Self-Love," he launches a bitter attack against the "selfish system of morals," among the modern proponents of which he singles out Hobbes and Locke:

> There is a principle, supposed to prevail among many, which is utterly incompatible with all virtue or moral sentiment; and as it can proceed from nothing but the most depraved disposition, so in its turn it tends still further to encourage that depravity. This principle is that *benevolence* is mere hypocrisy, friendship a cheat, public spirit a farce, fidelity a snare to procure trust and confidence; and that, while all of us, at bottom, pursue only our private interest, we wear these disguises in order to put others off their guard and expose them the more to our wiles and machinations. . . .
>
> There is another principle, somewhat resembling the former, which has been much insisted on by philosophers, and has been the foundation of many a system: that whatever affection one may feel or imagine he feels for others, no passion is or can be disinterested; that the most generous friendship, however sincere, is a modification of self-love; and that, even unknown to ourselves, we seek only our own gratification while we appear the most deeply engaged in schemes for the liberty and happiness of mankind.[36]
>
> Such a philosophy is more like a satyr than a true delineation or description of human nature, and may be a good foundation for paradoxical wit and raillery, but is a very bad one for any serious argument or reasoning.[37]

Thus, when Hume bases sympathy and sociality on self-concern, he seems to be joining Rousseau in warning against confusion between self-concern and selfishness, between ego and egoism, and, in a sense, to share Rousseau's distinction between *amour de soi* and *amour-propre*. *Amour de soi* or self-concern, rather than *amour-propre*, is man's most natural and primary quality; and there is no justification for concluding that because man has a natural "concern" for self he is fundamentally selfish,

---

36 Hume, "Of Self-Love," in *Hume's Moral and Political Philosophy*, ed. and introd. Henry D. Aiken (New York: Hafner Publishing Co., 1948), p. 270.
37 *Ibid.*, p. 275. The reference to Hobbes and Locke occurs on p. 271.

that because he has ego he is above all an egoist. Such a conclusion constitutes an unwarranted leap in logic. On the contrary,
self-concern is the basis of sympathy. In short, instead of arguing
that man's natural selfish egoism compels him toward a utilitarian sociality based on self-interest, Hume, like Rousseau, is arguing that man's primary concern for self is naturally "ejected" to
include others, so that concern for others becomes virtually one
with self-concern in the sentiment of sympathy, which for Hume
as for Rousseau is the source of all social virtues. In this sense,
sociality is grounded in consciousness itself.[38]

The problems that such a conception of sympathy pose for
Hume's philosophical system, however, are immediately apparent. The empiricism of that system would seem to preclude any
conception of the self other than that simple awareness that accompanies each of our sense impressions—and this is, in fact,
precisely the way in which Hume conceives of the self in the
section on personal identity in the *Treatise*.[39] Any conception of
the self as a distinct and constant "motif" or activity, any conception of the self as a positive state of mind, seems incompatible

---

38 In *The Phenomenology of the Social World*, Alfred Schutz disitnguishes
between our relations to other men as "fellow men" *(Mitmenschen)* and
our relations to them as "contemporaries" *(Nebenmenschen):* "We can say
that, living with my fellow men, I directly experience them and their subjective experiences. But of my contemporaries, we will say that, while living
among them, I do not immediately grasp their subjective experiences but
instead infer, on the basis of indirect evidence, the typical subjective experiences they must be having" (trans. G. Walsh and F. Lehnert [Evanston, Ill.:
Northwestern University Press], pp. 142–143). Perhaps this distinction between what one might call internalized and externalized "sympathy" corresponds in part to the differences between compassion or sympathy as
Rousseau and Hume conceive it, and other concepts of sociality, such as
those attacked by Hume. It is also worth comparing Schutz's description of
our experience of other men as *Nebenmenschen* with Locke's observation
in the *Essay*: ". . . no particular man can know the existence of any other
being, but only when, by actual operating on him, it makes itself perceived
by him": Bk. IV, chap. XI, art. 1. Perhaps even more relevant to our discussion, however, is the possibility of opposing *interest* and sympathy as
two very different principles of community—an opposition that will be
dealt with later.
39 Hume, *Treatise*, especially Bk. I, chap. ix, sect. vi, pp. 251–263.

with the sensationalism inherent especially in the earlier sections of the *Treatise* before the discussion of sympathy. And yet the concept of sympathy elaborated in the same work seems to demand a more "real," constant, and, so to speak, absolute self, distinct from particular sense impressions. As Hendel says,

> It is not surprising, then, that Hume should begin to question his own earlier account of the nature of the self, after finishing his last book on the system of the mind. Consciousness now loomed up before him with a reality that it had not possessed before. The person or self seemed more real than anything that enters our ken, despite our inability to seize upon any distinct perception of it. For it was only by admitting a greater initial impressiveness of the self, of which we are conscious, that we could explain how things and persons gain their importance or value from relation to ourselves, and evoke from us passionate sentiment.[40]

It is also not surprising that Hume in his later works abandons his attempt to account for the origin of sympathy. Instead of explicitly rejecting his earlier explanation, however, Hume quite simply admits to his doubts concerning the validity of his theory of mind and, with characteristic intellectual honesty, replaces his ambitious system with a philosophical skepticism even more profound than before. The bridge between the ambitions of the *Treatise* and the more modest products of his later skepticism is already provided by an appendix to the *Treatise,* added three years after the original; and here Hume makes it abundantly clear that the problem of the self is at the very heart of his philosophical doubts:

> I had entertain'd some hopes, that however deficient our theory of the intellectual world might be, it would be free from those contradictions, and absurdities, which seem to attend every explication, that human reason can give of the material world. But upon a more strict view of the section concerning personal identity, I find myself involved in such a labyrinth, that, I must confess, I neither know how to correct my former opinions, nor how to render them consistent. If this be not a good general reason for scepticism, 'tis at

40 Hendel, *op. cit.*, pp. 236–237.

least a sufficient one (if I were not already abundantly supplied) for me to entertain a diffidence and modesty in all my decisions.[41]

It is not difficult to understand why Hume is so uneasy about his authorship of the *Treatise*, despite the fact that it is considered by some to be his greatest work. To the extent that he maintains his views concerning sympathy and sociality as functions of self-consciousness, he must begin to question the most basic assumptions of the Lockean empiricist tradition in which, even with the modifications he introduced, he is usually included. If he does in fact abandon his explanation of sympathy, it is perhaps because he has been unable to devise a fundamentally new philosophical system that would, among other things, provide a basis for the necessary conception of self-consciousness. It may be that Kant is attempting to provide the very system that Hume needs, the very system that would support systematically the insights of both Hume and Rousseau.[42]

41 Hume, *Treatise*, p. 633.
42 At this point, it may be worth recalling our reasons for regarding Kant as the pivotal figure in the establishment of a new tradition in social and political thought, in opposition to that of Hobbes and Locke, despite the fact that certain important similarities exist between Kant's theory of "asocial sociability" and the conceptions of society here attributed to Hobbes and Locke. Since the problems of liberty and community are the central issues here, the fact that Kant's theory of mind provides the basis for a new conception of self, which is, in turn, the basis for different conceptions of liberty and community, would itself allow us to regard him as a turning point in social thought, even if some of his own social ideas seem to lag behind.

3. The Anthropological Dimension: Man and Society

> . . . even where we suppose that we have society before us in its empirically earliest and most primitive form, it is not something originally given but something spiritually conditioned and mediated. All social existence is rooted in concrete forms of community and of the feeling of community. And the more we succeed in laying bare this root, the more evident it becomes that the primary feeling of community never stops at the dividing lines which we posit in our highly developed biological class concepts but goes beyond them toward the totality of living things. Long before man had knowledge of himself distinguished by some specific power and singled out from nature as a whole by a specific primacy of value, he knew himself to be a link in the chain of life as a whole, within which each individual creature and thing is magically connected with the whole, so that a continuous transition, a metamorphosis of one being into another appears not only as possible but as necessary, as the "natural" form of life itself.
>
> ERNST CASSIRER
> *The Philosophy of Symbolic Forms: Myth*

The Passage from Nature to Culture

The concept of compassion which is central to Rousseau's discussion of individuation in the child also provides a key to his anthropology and his account of the passage from nature to culture. This transition involves a process similar to the one that culminates in ego-consciousness and fellow-feeling in the child. In the development of mankind, in a manner analogous to the development of individual men, there is a passage from an undifferentiated and unconscious community with all life to a differentiated consciousness of uniqueness and humanity. Again, this consciousness of his uniqueness and his humanity is the condition for man's union with other men, the condition for a con-

scious community of men. The process involved in this development is analogous to the "ejective" process involved in the birth
of compassion in children. In short, for Rousseau, the passage
from nature to culture is in effect the history of compassion in
mankind.

Lévi-Strauss, in his discussion of Rousseau referred to above,
while noting the importance for the nature-culture transition of
compassion and its union of intellectual and affective, interprets
its significance somewhat differently. According to Lévi-Strauss,
by defining man's natural condition in terms of his feeling of
compassion, Rousseau is able to account for the transition from
affectivity to intellectuality—which is here coterminous with the
transition from nature to culture—precisely because compassion
itself contains both an affective and an intellectual element.
Thus, all that is required to effect the transition is an act of
consciousness that translates affectivity into intellectuality. The
emergence of intellectuality is marked by man's ability to distinguish himself from others, first as a species and finally as an
individual. This ability gives rise to social differentiations, but
it would be impossible if man had not first learned to distinguish
among animal species. The transposition of distinctions among
animals to distinctions among men is based on man's prior feeling of identity with all animals.

To begin with, therefore, when Lévi-Strauss speaks of compassion he seems to be referring simply to the initial feeling of
identity with other animals that characterizes man in his natural
state. Compassion, in the sense of fellow-feeling, then, belongs
to man's preconscious and preintellectual condition, and this
"compassion" or identification, when translated into conscious
and intellectual form, results in social differentiation. Now, elsewhere in Lévi-Strauss's writings,[1] it seems clear that, as far as his
own ideas are concerned, he regards an act of differentiation as

---

[1] See, for example, Claude Lévi-Strauss, *The Savage Mind* (Chicago: University of Chicago Press, 1966), especially the discussions of totemism and
marriage practices.

also a principle of cohesion and unification in the mind of "primitive" man. But in this discussion of Rousseau, he leaves the impression that compassion simply means "unconscious" identification which, when it becomes conscious, results in differentiation—and the process stops there.

My own reading of Rousseau has led me to emphasize the dialectical process whereby unconscious identification with all life becomes, through a conscious ability to differentiate, a narrower, conscious form of compassion for other human creatures who are like oneself precisely because they are different from other animals. It is true that man's species-consciousness is the precondition for his ego-consciousness and individuality, but ego-consciousness is in turn the precondition for personal compassion. The process is dialectical, so that a principle of separation is always a new basis for community. Thus, I trace the dynamic of compassion one step further to its resolution in human community, and the transition from affectivity to intellectuality one step further to its resolution in a higher conscious affectivity —in short, to the conscious foundations of community. While Lévi-Strauss emphasizes compassion, in a broader sense of the word, for its contribution to social differentiation, I am emphasizing compassion, in a narrower sense, for its contribution to human community.

Here, then, is Rousseau's own account of man's emergence from his preconscious identity with all living beings to a consciousness of his own uniqueness and individuality and his ties with his fellow-men. After describing the conditions which led man into increased contact with other creatures and the necessities which taught him to use these creatures to his own advantage, Rousseau continues:

> This repeated relevance of various beings to himself, and of some to others, must naturally have engendered in the mind of man perceptions of certain relations. Those relations which we express by the words large, small, strong, weak, quick, slow, fearful, brave, and other similar ideas, compared whenever necessary and almost without thinking, finally produced in him some kind of reflection, or

rather a mechanical prudence which indicated to him the precautions most necessary to his safety.

The new insights that resulted from this development increased his superiority over other animals by making him conscious of it. . . . Thus, the first look that he turned upon himself produced the first stirring of pride; thus, hardly yet knowing how to distinguish among ranks, and considering himself in first rank as a member of his species, he prepared himself beforehand to claim that rank as an individual.

Although his fellow-men were not for him what they are for us, and though he hardly had more dealings with them than with other animals, they were not overlooked in his observations. The similarities that time allowed him to perceive among them, himself, and his female, allowed him to judge of those which he could not perceive; and seeing that they all conducted themselves just as he would have done in the same circumstances, he concluded that their manner of thinking and feeling conformed entirely to his own . . .[2]

This sequence of developments is clearly parallel to the evolution and consequences of self-awareness in the child. In the latter

---

[2] Jean-Jacques Rousseau, "Discours sur l'origine et les fondemens de l'inégalité parmi les hommes" (hereafter referred to as "Discours sur l'origine de l'inégalité") in *Œuvres Complètes* (Paris: Bibliothèque de la Pléiade, Gallimard, 1964), III, 165–166: "Cette application réitereé des êtres divers à lui-même, et des uns aux autres, dut naturellement engendrer dans l'esprit de l'homme les perceptions de certains rapports. Ces relations que nous exprimons par les mots de grand, de petit, de fort, de foible, de vite, de lent, de peureux, de hardi, et d'autres idées pareilles, comparées au besoin, et presque sans y songer, produisirent enfin chez lui quelque sorte de reflexion, ou plutot une prudence machinale qui lui indiquoit les precautions les plus necessaires à sa sureté.

"Les nouvelles lumières qui resulterent de ce développement augmentérent sa superiorité sur les autres animaux en la lui faisant connoître. . . . C'est ainsi qui le premier regard qu'il porta sur lui-même y produisit le premier mouvement d'orgueil; c'est ainsi que sachant encore à peine distinguer les rangs, et se contemplant au premier par son espèce, il se preparoit de loin à y prétendre par son individu.

"Quoique ses semblables ne fussent pas pour lui ce qu'ils sont pour nous, et qu'il n'eut guère plus de commerce avec eux qu'avec les autres animaux, ils ne furent pas oubliés dans ses observations. Les conformités que le temps put lui faire apercevoir entre eux, sa femelle et lui-même, lui firent juger de celles qu'il n'apercevoit pas, et, voyant qu'ils se conduisoient tous comme il aurait fait en pareilles circonstances, il conclut que leur manière de penser et de sentir étoit entièrement conforme à la sienne . . ."

case, Rousseau observes how a child becomes conscious of himself in the course of relations with the world around him and through the ways in which that world affects him. As he becomes conscious of himself, his instinctive "self-love" is translated into a sensitivity toward others, as soon as an awareness of his own nature allows him to see the similarities between his nature and that of the people around him. The process of differentiating himself from his environment joins him to others similarly differentiated. Analogously, "natural" man learns to distinguish himself from other creatures, as he makes use of them, and to take his unique position as man. But this distinction is clearly shared with other similar creatures, so that the act of consciousness that makes him a man simultaneously joins him with other men. His very ego-consciousness and individuality are functions of this consciousness of shared humanity. Again, the process of individuation is also a process of unification, and these two processes are inseparable in consciousness.

In achieving a consciousness of his humanity, which both separates him and binds him, man has made the transition from nature to culture. It is important to note, however, that this transition is not synonymous with the transition from the "state of nature" to civil society. The transition from nature to culture, from unconscious universal "community" to conscious human community is prior to and distinct from the future establishment of civil society and the subsequent political order. In other words, there is a human community prior to civil society—a community that is an internal necessity and not an arrangement based on contract. This community would not be a sufficient condition for the establishment of contractual society, which becomes necessary for reasons of prudence. In fact, according to Rousseau civil society as it has been historically instituted has tended to violate and destroy any natural sense of community, and this is why it becomes necessary to establish a new form of social contract, one in accord with true community.

Man's capacity to think himself part of a human community,

indeed his natural tendency to unite in consciousness his own individuality and his unity with others, may be what makes Rousseau's ideal of the social contract possible and his concept of the general will meaningful. Rousseau himself seems to think that if men were joined in community only by material self-interest and the desire for physical comfort, this concept would be nothing more than the vaguest abstraction. But Rousseau expressly denies that it is self-interest alone that compels men to remain united in the common good:

> Everyone, it is said, concurs with the public good for his own interest. But how is it then that the just man will concur with it to his own prejudice? What does it mean to go to one's death for one's interest? . . .
>
> . . . [The natural] sentiments, as far as the individual is concerned, are self-love, the fear of pain, the horror of death, the desire for well-being. But if, as cannot be doubted, man is sociable by nature, or at least made to become sociable, he can only be so by virtue of other innate sentiments, inherent in his species; for, if only physical need is considered, it would certainly disperse men rather than unite them.[3]

Instead, the principle of community and the common good are man's natural fellow-feeling and *conscience,* which is innate.[4] Conscience is, in effect, man's ability to feel the general will as part of himself, and that ability is a function of his capacity to feel and think himself one with his fellow-men.

The true social contract based on the concept of the general will operates by allowing man's feelings and behavior to

---

[3] Rousseau, *Emile,* in *Oeuvres Complètes,* IV, 599–600: "Chacun, dit-on, concourt au bien publique pour son intérêt. Mais d'ou vient donc que le juste y concourt à son préjudice? Qu'est-ce qu'aller à la mort pour son intérêt? . . .

". . . Ces sentiments, quant à l'individu, sont l'amour de soi, la crainte de la douleur, l'horreur de la mort, le désir du bien-être. Mais si, comme on n'en peut douter, l'homme est sociable par sa nature, ou du moins fait pour le devenir, il ne peut l'être que par d'autres sentiments innés, relatifs à son espèce; car, à ne considerer que le besoin physique, il doit certainement disperser les hommes au lieu de les rapprocher."

[4] *Ibid.*

conform to the demands of his natural consciousness—to his "species-consciousness," if we may borrow the Marxist term. In other words, it institutionalizes the natural process of "ejection" toward which consciousness tends. Rousseau's objection to civil society as it actually has been constituted is, in a sense, that it violates the fundamental community of men and tends to alienate man's sentiments from their conscious foundations. It is possible, Rousseau believes, so to construct society as to separate men from each other in sentiment by institutionalizing their separateness and fostering antagonism, as does the egoistic, grossly unequal, and competitive society of Hobbes and Locke. Historically, in fact, civil society has been so constituted. The ideal society for Rousseau is one that, as it were, institutionalizes *compassion.*

At this point, perhaps it should be re-emphasized that Rousseau's ideas on the transition from nature to culture ought not to be confused with his ideas on the passage from the state of nature to the civil state.[5] The transition referred to in *The Social Contract* (Book I, Chap. VIII) is simply the one from the state of nature to the civil state. The *other* one—the passage from nature to culture—is discussed in the *Discourse on the Origins of Inequality,* particularly near the beginning of Part II. While the transition to civil society may be regarded as a moral one, this anthropological transition is more primary, involving a transformation in consciousness. In other words, the passage from nature to culture is the evolution of human consciousness, the development of self-consciousness—man's consciousness of his humanity and, subsequently, of his individuality. The important point, too, is that this development of consciousness is inseparable from *compassion,* which is, in effect, the dialectical

5 We are here using "nature-culture" in the modern anthropological sense—as does Lévi-Strauss—and applying it to a development that Rousseau describes without, of course, using this terminology. Lévi-Strauss uses the terminology in his discussion of Rousseau precisely to emphasize the importance of Rousseau's insight into an anthropological problem which he recognized, even if he did not name it.

source of self-consciousness and the basis of the union of individuality and community. Since the passage from nature to culture can simply be regarded as the emergence of man as man, an understanding of Rousseau's conception of this development is crucial to an understanding of his concept of human nature, particularly his conception of the relationship between individuality and sociality.

It is also important not to confuse community, as a fact of consciousness, with society, as empirical social relations, *or* either one with civil society. Man in the precivil "state of nature" is *social* for both Rousseau and Locke. For Rousseau, however, the state of nature is characterized not only by social relations, but also by a fundamental development in human consciousness—which is what makes man distinctively human. His conception of human consciousness leads to a particular idea of *community* —community as a fact of consciousness, community as, so to speak, a category of consciousness, at least as primary as individuality and inseparable from it—which man brings to social experience and through which he renders experience intelligible. This concept of community in turn necessarily affects Rousseau's idea of society and the possibilities of social relations.[6]

For Rousseau, then, the historical "contract" that actually put an end to the factual state of nature—an agreement that was a contract of government rather than a true social compact—*violated* human sociality by institutionalizing acquisitiveness, competition, and a struggle for power. The ideal *social* contract that Rousseau prescribes would re-establish true sociality by institutionalizing natural compassion and the sense of community. The transition from the state of nature to civil society is quite differ-

[6] To put it another way, one might refer to Lévi-Strauss's suggestion about the development of a distinctively human social life: certain things have to be conceptualized in order to be lived. One might say that, for Rousseau, the passage from nature to culture took place when the feeling of community with all life became conscious, was conceptualized, and, by being conceptualized, made possible the dialectical process of differentiation and individuation—the bases of human social life. See Lévi-Strauss, *op. cit.*, pp. 99–100.

ent for both Hobbes and Locke. In almost every respect, for them contract *is* the principle of sociality.[7] Man passes from nature to society with no fundamental change occurring in him as a precondition to this passage. Just as in the history of individual "consciousness," ego remains the constant, unchangeable factor, so the common denominator of the historical state of nature and civil society—even the ideal civil society—is the egoistic individualism inherent in the psychology of natural man. Civil society is what it is precisely because man remains fundamentally the same throughout.

This idea of the continuity of human nature represents an important difference between the social thought of Hobbes and Locke, on the one hand, and Rousseau, on the other. Civil society, for Rousseau, is based on a very clear antecedent passage from nature to culture that involves a clear change in human psychology. This change is a precondition for *any* uniquely human form of society; and the natural evolution of consciousness and compassion whereby man achieves community with other men provides Rousseau with a standard for his *ideal* society.

Hobbes and Locke, however, seem to have no such conception of a dynamic, evolving human nature or consciousness—no conception of a higher consciousness at all—which is essentially different in the state of nature from what it is in society. In other words, for all practical purposes, there is no nature-culture dualism at the heart of their social doctrine.[8] And having already begun with a conception of natural man as consciously

7 This statement and the argument that follows are, of course, not self-evident. Certainly there are commentators who would disagree most profoundly with the view that, at least in Locke's case, there is no extra-societal community. I shall develop this argument and deal with an opposing view in the section on sociality.

8 There is, if anything, a distinction between prepolitical and political. The significant point, however, is that the nature of man, his consciousness, etc., is always a constant factor. It also may be worth considering C. B. Macpherson's argument in *The Political Theory of Possessive Individualism* (Oxford: Clarendon Press, 1962) that Locke's state of nature is itself simply abstracted from existing civil society.

and deliberately egoistic from the start, they are forced to take him into civil society in virtually the same condition, placing very little between egoistic man and social man but contracts based on prudence, a desire for security, and coercion. For both Hobbes and Locke, man's identity as man seems to rest on his primary, irreducible, and constant egoism; while for Rousseau, man's humanity is the culmination of a process in which his consciousness of himself and of his manhood is inseparable from his consciousness of community with other men.[9]

These anthropological differences have important implications. It is clear that views on what constitutes the good society are likely to differ according to what is regarded as distinctively human. Thus, just as Rousseau's good society, based on a true social contract, can be regarded as an institutionalization of the compassion and sense of community inherent in his dynamic concept of human nature, Locke's doctrine of property and a civil society based on the right of property can be looked upon as an institutionalization of his psychology of acquisitive egoism.

A brief word about Kant is perhaps in order here. Inasmuch as a certain philosophical approach is being characterized in terms of a nature-culture dualism and a dynamic conception of human nature and consciousness, it may seem particularly strange that this approach should be associated with Kant, who is often accused of having no real historical perspective and a static view of the human mind. Nevertheless, the dialectical quality of Kant's approach has been stressed here from the outset, for example in his treatment of the subject-object problem and the development of self-consciousness. It is interesting to note, therefore, that Kant remained faithful to this dynamic outlook even in his scanty and relatively undeveloped writings on history, and that his dialectical approach to the subject-object problem is maintained in his historical anthropology.

[9] It might be worth noting that such modern anthropologists as Lévi-Strauss and David Bidney have been impressed by Rousseau's anthropology and his insight into the nature-culture problem.

One significant quotation from Kant's "Conjectural Beginning of Human History" should be sufficient to illustrate this point, and also several others which have been raised with regard to the Kantian approach to the individual-community problem:

> The fourth and last step taken by reason which raises man completely above community with animals was that man realized (however obscurely) that he is actually the end of Nature, and that nothing living on earth could compete with him in this respect. The first time he said to the sheep: "The skin which you wear was given to you by Nature, not for yourself, but for me," when he removed that skin and put it on himself, then he became aware of the privilege which he had over all animals by virtue of his nature; and he no longer looked upon these animals as fellow-creatures, but as means and tools granted him for the attainment of whatever goals he pleased. This idea entails (however obscurely) the notion of contrast: that he may not say such a thing to any human being, but must regard men as equal participants in the gifts of Nature. This was an early preparation for the restrictions which reason would later impose on his will with regard to his fellow-men, a preparation which is much more necessary to the establishment of society than affection and love.[10]

10 Immanuel Kant, "Muthmasslicher Anfang der Menschengeschichte," in *Gesammelte Schriften* (Berlin and Leipzig: Prussian Academy of Sciences, 1910–), VIII, 114: "Der vierte und letzte Schritt, den die den Menschen über die Gesellschaft mit Thieren ganzlich erhebende Vernunft that, war: dass er (wiewohl nur dunkel) begriff, er sei eigentlich der Zweck der Natur, und nichts, was auf Erden lebt, könne hierin einen Mitwerber gegen ihn abgeben. Das erstemal, dass er zum Schafe sagte: den Pelz den du trägst, hat dir die Natur nicht für dich, sondern für mich gegeben, ihm ihn abzog und sich selbst anlegte: ward er eines Vorrechtes inne, welches er vermöge seiner Natur über alle Thiere hatte, die er nun nicht mehr als seine Mitgenossen an der Schöpfung, sondern also seinem Willen überlassene Mittel und Werkzeuge zu Erreichung seiner beliebingen Absichten ansah. Diese Vorstellung schliesst (wiewohl dunkel) den Gedanken des Gegensatzes ein: dass er so etwas zu keinem Menschen sagen durfe, sondern diesen als gleichen Thielnehmer an den Geschenken der Natur anzusehen habe; eine Vorbereitung von weitem zu den Einschränkungen, die die Vernunft künftig dem Willen in Ansehung seines Mitmenschen auferlegen sollte, und welche weit mehr als Zuneigung und Liebe zu Errichtung der Gesellschaft notwending ist."

This is perhaps also the place to mention the fact that Kant himself sug-

This account of man's emergence from the natural state is strikingly similar to that of Rousseau. Here again the process begins with man's original identification with all animals. In the course of man's utilization of other creatures for his own comfort, that undifferentiated community with all life yields to man's ability to distinguish himself from other animals; and, again, that ability is the condition both for his own consciousness of self and for his identification and community with other men. Once more the process of differentation is also a process of unification; individuality and community are inseparable, and consciousness of self and humanity are social phenomena. Human community is grounded in an act of consciousness—a consciousness that is dialectical, both with respect to its dynamic

---

gests a particularly intriguing mode of connecting the problems of freedom or, more specifically, creative individuality, and community. Kant clearly states his conviction that in man's creative instinct lies an essential—if not *the* essential—source of sociability, since this creative instinct, expressed particularly in the aesthetic sence, is accompanied by the capacity *and* the desire to communicate and share pleasure. Indeed, according to Kant, we judge man to be civilized and sociable insofar as he ". . . is inclined and able to communicate his pleasure to others and . . . is not satisfied with any object if he cannot feel delight in it in community with others." (*The Critique of Judgment*, trans. and introd. by J. H. Bernard [New York: Hafner Publishing Co., 1957], p. 297, art. 41.)

Moreover, "one cannot avoid regarding taste as a faculty of judging everything whereby one can communicate even a feeling to everyone else, and consequently as a means of promoting that which everyone's natural inclination demands," that is, sociability and communication. (*Ibid.*)

Thus, man's aesthetic judgment, reflecting his ability to communicate feelings as well as conceptual thought, is in an important sense the essence of his sociability. To put it another way, the conditions for art and the conditions for society are essentially the same with respect to the qualities in human nature which produce them; and both, while they are the conditions for man's individual creative self-development, are the embodiments of man's natural sociability and the natural community of men: "The propaedeutic to all beautiful art, as far as its highest grade of perfection is concerned, apparently lies not in precepts but in the cultivation of the mental powers by means of those elements of knowledge called humanities—probably because humanity signifies, on the one hand, the general feeling of sympathy, and on the other hand, the capacity to communicate our deepest selves universally. These qualities bound together constitute man's characteristic sociability, whereby he differentiates himself from animal limitations." (*Ibid*, p. 355, art. 60).

quality and its union of opposites. Finally, here too society is ultimately based on this achievement of consciousness that gives man his unique identity, first as species and then as individual, while at the same time uniting him in community with other men.

The Neo-Kantian Ernst Cassirer pursues these various themes more explicitly and exhaustively in his writings on myth. Cassirer regards myth as an expression of human consciousness, a source of fundamental spiritual categories through which man gives form to the "raw material" supplied by the otherwise meaningless and chaotic elements of his physical and social existence. The history of myth, then, in a sense represents the history of consciousness.

Cassirer emphasizes that mythical consciousness is not simply derivative from man's social life, but is rather one of the conditions for that life, operating as one means of spiritual synthesis that establishes a relationship between "I" and "thou," individual and community. Myth is "an instrument of the great process of spiritual differentiation through which basic determinate forms of social and individual consciousness arise from the chaos of the first indeterminate life feeling." [11] This process of spiritual differentiation which is the basis of human social life is both a process of increasing individuation—from the community of all life to species-consciousness to individuality—and at the same time a process of unification into new forms of community. Social consciousness and individual consciousness are inseparable and reciprocal:

> First of all, the development of myth shows one thing very clearly; even the most universal form of the human consciousness of kind, even the manner in which man differentiates himself from the totality of biological forms and groups himself with his fellow men into a natural species, is not given from the beginning as a *starting point* of the mythical-religious world view but should be understood rather

11 Ernst Cassirer, *The Philosophy of Symbolic Forms* (New Haven: Yale University Press, 1966), II, 178.

as a mediated product, a result of this very world view. For the mythical-religious consciousness the limits of the species "man" are not rigid but thoroughly fluid. Only by a progressive concentration, only by a gradual narrowing of that universal life-feeling in which myth originates, does it gradually arrive at the specifically human feeling of community.[12]

The primary fact of mythical-religious consciousness, then, is a feeling of community; community is prior to individuality in the development of consciousness. This feeling of community and the fluid relationships that it establishes between self and other are fundamental to the logic of mythical consciousness; and, ultimately, human society rests on this logic:

> The very existence and form of human society itself requires such a foundation; for even where we suppose that we have society before us in its empirically earliest and most primitive form, it is not something originally given but something spiritually conditioned and mediated. All social existence is rooted in concrete forms of community and of the feeling of community.[13]

Thus, a sense of community is a condition for society, and community is grounded in consciousness; community is, in fact, a category of consciousness, a category that renders social life intelligible and distinctively human.

The fluidity that characterizes the relationship between man and animal also characterizes the relationship between individual men and the human group. At first, ". . . the individual consciousness remains confined within the tribe consciousness and dissolves into it." [14] But when the next "crisis" of individuation occurs, by which man achieves a specific consciousness of his "I," it again becomes a new principle of community. For example, when Greek tribal gods are replaced by Homer's personal gods, the latter are also the first national gods of the Greeks. In this way, the first mythical-religious expression of personal con-

---

12 *Ibid.*
13 *Ibid.*, p. 194.
14 *Ibid.*, p. 199.

sciousness is also the first expression of the universal Hellenic consciousness, and the tribal or group community gives way to both a more specific individuality and a more comprehensive community. Therefore, with every "trend toward the individual is bound up a new tendency toward the universal—which is only seemingly in conflict with it and in truth is correlative to it." [15]

The Nature of Human Sociality

Clearly, whatever their views on individuality or the passage from nature to culture, all thinkers are faced with the inescapable fact of man's social existence, which must be somehow accounted for. At this point in the discussion, then, we must deal more explicitly wth the question of what constitutes human sociality.

The difficulty of this question varies, of course, according to the degree of antagonism to society that any view of individuality entails. Hobbes provides the clearest and most straightforward solution to the problem of placing into society men who are naturally egoistic, aggressive, and competitive and who "have no pleasure (but on the contrary a great deale of griefe) in keeping company, where there is no power able to over-awe

[15] *Ibid.* One cannot help being struck by the fact that, although Cassirer himself, in his *The Question of Jean-Jacques Rousseau,* denies that Rousseau attributes to man an innate principal of sociability, his own conception of human sociability is so much like that of Rousseau. In connection with Cassirer's remarks on the growing comprehensiveness of the community, coupled with growing individuality, in the evolution of Greek religion, there is another point worth noting by way of again drawing together our two themes of freedom and community. The evolution of the Greek gods also represented the development of a new morality—the morality of the free self-conscious and self-active rational will and of responsibility, as opposed to the old morality of blood vengeance, the morality, as it were, of biological necessity, stimulus and response, determined by overwhelming external forces (the Moirai, the Erinyes, etc.). Thus, the new gods may represent both a new community of men, overriding the enmities of family and clan antagonisms, *and* a new consciousness of freedom based on the triumph of human reason and its mastery, at least partial, over previously uncontrolled forces, a new individuality that is at the same time the essence of a new community. Greek conceptions of the polis often seem quite deliberately to unite these two themes by making this new form of community represent

them all." [16] Hobbes simply attributes to man a prudence and love of security which drive him into society with others for the sake of peace and order, and which compel him to support his frail wisdom by establishing that coercive "power able to over-awe them all." Civil society need not be based on any prior sense of community, but only on contract supported by coercion and by religious and educational systems—which apparently also rest ultimately on some form of coercion.

Locke presents a somewhat more complicated picture. He seeks to moderate Hobbes' rather catastrophic view of man's unsociability and its disastrous consequences for his natural condition; and hence he seems to deny Hobbes' unequivocal statements to the effect that man is not a social creature. Nevertheless, what Locke means when he says that man is naturally a social being is problematic, to say the least.

In order to clarify my own interpretation of Locke's conception of human sociality, I shall deal with an opposing interpretation, one that emphasizes the natural community of men in Locke's doctrine and argues that, for Locke, individuality and sociality are inseparable.

In *La politique morale de John Locke,* Raymond Polin seeks to deny claims that Locke's philosophy is one of radical individualism by arguing that for Locke individuality and sociality are not only compatible but inseparable. Polin's contention, quite simply, is that, Locke's man having been born free and

---

the triumph of human reason and freedom over the dark forces of nature. This may, for example, be the significance of Aeschylus' trilogy, *Oresteia,* in which only the polis, in the person of Athena, is able to break the endless "natural" cycle of blood vengeance, to transform the Erinyes into the Eumenides, by replacing the bloody retribution of the Furies with the human—and humane—justice of the polis, represented here by the court of the Areopagus. Cf. Richard Kuhn, *The House, the City and the Judge: The Growth of Moral Awareness in the Oresteia* (Indianapolis and New York: Bobbs-Merrill Co., 1962) and George Thomson, *Aeschylus and Athens* (New York: Universal Library, Grosset and Dunlap, 1968), just to cite two examples of similar arguments about the meaning of the *Oresteia.*

16 Thomas Hobbes, *Leviathan* (Oxford: Clarendon Press, 1909), p. 95 (chap. 13).

rational, ". . . it is the same rational freedom that creates both the individuality and the sociability of man, that constitutes both the principle of individuality and the principle of sociality." [17]

To explain the nature of this unity of individuality and sociality, Polin first points to the connection between *reason* and individuality in Locke's doctrine. He begins with the observation that for Locke the identity and individuality of a rational being are a function of the consciousness that accompanies all thought. Freedom, which is so much a part of individuality, is itself a function of rational thought, and hence of consciousness. Thus, it is only a rational being who can be regarded as truly an individual, just as only such a being can be truly free. Individuality, then, is defined in terms of the *right* of freedom and the related right of property, and the *obligation* to obey the laws of reason, an obligation that is the essence of rationality.

Having thus established the intimate relationship between reason and individuality, Polin turns to the passages in Locke's *Second Treatise* indicating that reason is a bond that unites men into a natural community, a community that would suffice them if only degenerate and corrupt men did not exist.[18] Reason is the basis of sociability in that it establishes a social obligation; and just as reason is an essential property of man's humanity, so is sociability. Thus, since individuality and sociability are alike grounded in reason, they are compatible and inseparable. Men are individuals only insofar as they are free and rational; and insofar as they are free and rational, they are sociable.

But—and this turns out to be the crucial point:

[17] Raymond Polin, *La politique morale de John Locke* (Paris: Presses Universitaires de France, 1960), p. 138: ". . . c'est la même liberté raisonnable qui fait à la fois l'individualité de l'homme et sa sociabilité, qui constitue à la fois le principe de l'individu et le principe du social."

[18] See, for example, John Locke, *The Second Treatise,* in *Two Treatises of Government,* ed. Peter Laslett (New York: Mentor Books, 1965), pp. 397 and 429 (arts. 128 and 172).

The sociability to which man is destined by God is not the product of a necessary development, but *the contingent and hypothetical product of human freedom confronted with a rational obligation.* God created man to be a sociable individual, but he left him free to realize or not to realize his individuality, to fulfill or not to fulfill his sociability. Individuality and sociability are essential obligations for man, and are moreover perfectly compatible and consistent, but they are only obligations, that is, *necessities of a purely moral nature.*[19]

It is clear now that "individuality," "sociability," and even "reason," are being used here in a normative sense. And this is precisely the point. Sociability, in the sense intended here, is a moral principle, not a psychological fact. It is perhaps a Law of Nature rather than a law of human nature. A similar statement can be made about reason. Reason—with a capital R—is the great *as if* of Locke's moral and political philosophy. It is a principle of obligation rather than a description of human nature. Locke's writings give ample testimony to his own lack of faith in *actual* human rationality. As a political principle, this doctrine of Reason simply establishes the principle that all mature men are to be treated and judged responsible *as if* endowed with divine Reason. This principle defines the rights and the limitations on those rights of man in his relation to the state and provides a guideline for the legitimate use of coercive power by the state. One ought not to forget that *The Second Treatise* is above all a work on power and its legitimate uses, and that the need for coercive power is based on the disparity between human psychology and the demands of Reason.

It might also be worth noting that the state of nature in which

---

[19] Polin, *op. cit.*, p. 135 (emphasis added): "La sociabilité à laquelle Dieu a destiné l'individu humain n'est donc pas le produit d'un développement essentiel, mais l'oeuvre aléatoire et hypothètique d'une liberté humaine affrontée à une obligation raisonnable. Dieu a fait l'homme pour qu'il soit un individu sociable, mais il a laissé à sa liberté le soin de réaliser ou de ne pas réaliser son individualité, d'accomplir ou de ne pas accomplir sa sociabilité. Individualité et sociabilité sont pour l'homme des obligations essentielles, et d'ailleurs parfaitement compatibles et accordées, mais ce sont seulement des obligations, c'est à dire des exigences d'ordre purement moral."

Reason and its correlative sociability are operative is itself a normative construct. In fact, Polin himself criticizes Leo Strauss—and others—for failing to recognize the dual character of Locke's state of nature and to distinguish between the normative state of nature and the historical state of nature. In his criticism of Strauss, moreover, Polin makes a point which is particularly significant for this discussion of Locke's psychology:

> Because of his failure to distinguish between the theoretical state of nature and the factual state of nature, Leo Strauss . . . attempts to liken the Lockean conception to the catastrophic conception of the state of nature made famous by Hobbes. . . . On this point, Hobbes and Locke have in common only the theme of human frailty and "wickedness."[20]

Thus, Polin himself distinguishes between man's normative "nature" and his actual nature; and the very theme Locke and Hobbes have in common—the one Polin so lightly dismisses—is the crucial point here. It is clear from the references to man's "frailty and wickedness" that human psychology is hardly a mirror of divine Reason. We have already noted the prominent place given by Locke to possessiveness and the love of power and dominion in the psychology of children. One might also take this occasion to distinguish between Reason and reason, and to point out the similarities between Locke's and Hobbes's conceptions of the latter as a calculating faculty ideally operating in the interests of egoism.[21]

Sociability, for Locke, then, characterizes the theoretical state of nature; egoism, the factual state of nature;[22] and civil society

---

[20] *Ibid.*, p. 176, n. 4: "Faute d'avoir distingué entre état théorique de nature et état de nature de fait, M. Leo Strauss . . . s'efforce de rapprocher la conception lockienne de la conception catastrophique de l'état de nature mise en honneur par Hobbes. . . . Sur ce point, Hobbes et Locke n'ont en commun que le thème de la fragilité et de la 'mauvaiseté' humaines."

[21] See, for example, Hobbes, *op. cit.*, chaps. 5, 13, 14; and Locke, *An Essay Concerning Human Understanding*, ed. A. C. Fraser (New York: Dover Books, 1959), Vol. I, esp. p. 348 (Bk. II, chap. xxi, art. 52).

[22] This should not be taken to mean that there are no social relations in the state of nature. For a discussion of one sense in which Locke may be said to

is entered into precisely because, in the historical state of nature, human egoism proved to be rather incompatible with the rational obligation of sociability. Despite Polin's efforts to establish certain fundamental differences between Hobbes and Locke, he could as easily have argued that individuality and sociability are compatible for Hobbes; for in spite of his ideas concerning the natural unsociability of men—ideas not so very different from Locke's conception of man's actual nature—Hobbes also has a normative concept of natural Reason as a guide to natural law and a basis for social existence.

There is also another perspective to this problem of distinguishing between the real and the ideal in Locke. We have already discussed the sense in which human sociability can be regarded as grounded in Reason; but Polin's argument is somewhat more complicated. In order to deny Locke's radical individualism, Polin is not satisfied to establish the sociability of rational man. More significantly, he tries to establish an intimate connection between sociability and individuality, arguing that according to Locke one is a function of the other. It will be remembered that, to establish this connection, Polin begins with an observation that individuality is a function of consciousness —the consciousness that accompanies all thought—and hence, apparently, of rational thought. Therefore, if individuality, like sociability, is grounded in Reason, clearly the two are inseparable as common functions of Reason.

There is a problem here, however. It has already been noted that the Reason that is the principle of sociality is reason in its normative sense and, as such, has very little to do with the simple "consciousness that accompanies all thought." It is scarcely legitimate, then, to conclude that individuality and sociability are together grounded in Reason simply because individuality is a function of consciousness. Either individuality and sociabil-

attribute a kind of natural sociality to men, insofar as he "discovers" society as a self-subsistent entity independent of political order, see below, pp. 105–108.

ity in Locke's doctrine are not as intimately related as Polin contends they are, or individuality also has a dual meaning—as even some of Polin's own language would suggest: a normative meaning, insofar as it is grounded in Reason; and a factual, psychological meaning, insofar as it is grounded in consciousness.

Moreover, it can be argued that consciousness as Locke conceives it has very little to do with reason even in its ordinary sense, let alone in its exalted normative sense. We have already discussed Locke's epistemology with respect to his conception of "the consciousness that accompanies all thought," to which Polin refers. It will be remembered that Locke often uses "thought" interchangeably with "perception" and thus defines consciousness as simply the perception of perception. In his explanation of the relationship between consciousness and personal identity, Locke refers to "that consciousness which is inseparable from thinking, and, as it seems to me, essential to it, it being impossible for anyone to perceive without *perceiving* that he does perceive." [23] Thought or perception in this context is simply that "modification" of the mind "which actually accompanies and is annexed to, any impression on the body, made by an external object" and "furnishes the mind with a distinct idea, which we call *sensation*." [24] Therefore, consciousness is simply the direct and immediate awareness of sensation, and not a distinct act of mind achieved only at a higher level of mental activity. An infant, insofar as it is aware of sense impressions—can feel hot or cold, for example—is apparently conscious in this sense. If consciousness has anything to do with reason, it is only with reason in a very rudimentary sense, and certainly not reason in the sense of a fulfilled rationality. If reason is the basis of individuality, it is individuality in some normative sense. Psychological "individuality," the *ego*, the individuality that is grounded in consciousness, is a simple, primary, irreducible phenomenon, as basic and as easily "achieved" as sensation itself.

[23] Locke, *Essay*, I, p. 449 (Bk. II, chap. xxvii, art. 11).
[24] *Ibid.*, p. 299 (Bk. II, chap. xix, art. 1).

It neither requires sociality to effectuate it, nor does it in turn foster sociality. If anything, this fundamental individuality, this ultimate primary ego-consciousness must be subdued to achieve sociality. It is this fundamental individuality that concerns us in any discussion of Locke's view on human psychology; and, as shall be argued in what follows, it is actually this psychology itself, rather than pure Reason, that in a sense provides Locke with his ultimate normative standard and acts as the focal point of his political doctrine.

There is no question, to begin with, that a fundamental conflict exists between Locke's psychological assumptions and his moral premises. Psychologically, men are isolated from and perhaps even repelled by each other.[25] For moral and religious purposes, they must be conceived of as members of a community, united in the pursuit of a common good. The question here is how Locke resolves the conflict between these two sets of assumptions for the purpose of his political doctrine, whether he resolves it in favor of the moral principle or the psychological one. If one could in fact establish that, his views on human psychology notwithstanding, Locke *prescribes* sociality and the inseparability of individuality and true sociality as his ultimate norms or values, Polin's claims could, at least in part, be sustained; but it is precisely this that the present argument denies, suggesting instead that the psychology of individualism becomes a political norm—and one that runs counter to the rational norm of community. It is true that "possessive individualism" represents for Locke a *failure*—a failure to suppress the "vicious" qualities that emerge so early and inevitably in human nature— in earliest infancy, as we have already seen. In this sense, the

25 It has been suggested to me that this conflict can be regarded as the opposition of a utilitarian psychology, according to which the *avoidance* of *pain* (or in Locke's case, "uneasiness") is the only certain motive upon which a theory of behavior can be based, to a moral theory which is based on the premise that men are *attracted* to the *good*—specifically the morally good. Thus, psychologically, men would "avoid" each other as inflicters of pain, while for religious and moral purposes they would be regarded as united in the pursuit of a common good.

natural vices are for Locke sinful, inasmuch as they violate the "natural" community ("natural" in a different sense) ordained by God—the community that seems so central to Locke's religious and moral convictions. It may, then, seem misleading to suggest, as C. B. Macpherson has done, that Locke somehow *advocates* "possessive individualism." Nevertheless, if the argument here is not quite as unequivocal on this point as is Macpherson's, it will still be maintained that ultimately, in Locke's social and political thought, his *descriptive* account of man as ego-assertive "possessive individualist" *supersedes* his moral and religious principles, not simply as a more realistic account of man, but as a standard upon which civil society is to be judged. I shall try to show, particularly by examining Locke's use of the state-of-nature device, that his political order is based on the psychological principle, not simply in the sense that the political order must accommodate itself to the realities of human frailty, or must contain man's antisocial "vices" to an extent consonant with liberty, but rather in the sense that that civil order is most just that best corresponds to, indeed allows the expression of, the acquisitive and competitive individualism of man's true nature —that is, a civil order firmly based on property differentials and class relations.

What is being suggested, then, is that just as Locke, like the liberal tradition that follows him, removes religion from the political realm together with other individual "rights" and grounds it firmly in man's "private" existence, so does he remove the communal principle associated with that religion from his conception of man's concrete social and political existence—as it were, "privatizes" it. The invisible community of believers that remains, whatever else it may be, is not for Locke the essence of mundane social or political relations. It does not significantly counteract the social manifestations of man's psychological nature, nor—more importantly for us—does it even provide the basis for Locke's political prescriptions, except possibly in a very attenuated sense. In the political realm, this community is replaced by a new abstract, and in effect fictional, community objectified in the form of the state as the coercive representative of the "common interest." If the moral community continues to play a role in the political sphere, it is, ironically, in a form tailored to the demands of this abstract political community and the psychological conditions on which it is based. On the one hand, the rational "sociality" of Locke's moral doctrine is simply reflected in his commonwealth in the sense that a principle of legitimacy is necessary to justify the use of power to maintain order and security—conditions that often require the sacrifice of individual desires to the common interest, and therefore often require coercion. In this sense, Locke's "sociality" is really nothing more than the minimum condition for any political order. On the other hand, of course, as a principle of political legitimacy the notion of a moral community of free and rational men must also establish the *limits* within which that state can act. But even in this sense Locke's "moral community" does little more than establish a principle that would hardly be foreign to his liberal successors, who complete the dissociation of the moral community from social and political life— the utilitarians who factor out the religious dimension altogether. If in Locke the religious perspective is still strong, one ought not to allow it to obscure the fact that in the political realm his idea of the moral community is profoundly conditioned by his conception of actual social relations and the psychological assumptions that underlie that conception.[26]

26 Certain commentators, like Peter Laslett, have argued that there is a contradiction, or at least a lack of congruence, between Locke's epistemological and psychological work—specifically the *Essay Concerning Human Understanding*—and his political theory. It can, however, be said that if there is a conflict in Locke's work, it is not between the *Essay* and the political doctrine, but rather within the political theory itself. The contradiction, if it exists at all, is between the conception of social life and the political prescriptions, on the one hand, and the moral and religious doctrine on the other, both of which appear in the political theory. Without the religious doctrine—and it has been argued here that the latter is not, except in the most severely modified form, a principle of social and political significance

The significance of Locke's actual conception of human psychology, as distinct from his ideal conception of man's moral nature, becomes clear when it is examined in the context of the state of nature. The state of nature is human nature writ large; and, as was pointed out earlier, just as there are an actual and an ideal human nature, there are corresponding actual and ideal states of nature—what one might call a psychological state and a moral state. The ideal conception of the state of nature describes a world populated by men who conform to their ideal moral natures; the actual state of nature describes a world populated by men as they *are*, only without government and legal order. One might expect the moral description to serve as the norm for Locke's political prescriptions. If this were so, it would, of course, deny the role that the present argument attributes to Locke's psychology of individualism. The point, however, is precisely that the actual, psychological state of nature provides a moral standard for Locke's political prescriptions, and it is in this sense that the psychology of individualism becomes the moral basis of his good society.

—the congruence between the political theory of *The Second Treatise*, for example, and the psychology of the *Essay* is much more readily apparent.

This connection between the political theory and the psychology cannot help but raise again the question of which came first. The fact is that Locke at least *wrote* about political problems first, his earliest works having been concerned with the problems of toleration and natural law; only much later did he develop a theory of epistemology and psychology, or a conception of individuality and the self. If one regards this sequence as reflective of Locke's thought process, suggesting that he tended to read political life back into all experience, it does seem to clarify certain matters. For example, it might help to explain why, despite the fact that Locke—as well as Hobbes—believed that man's most primitive existence is "sociable" in the sense that it is characterized by family life, nevertheless he maintained his view of the individual as an ego asserting itself against society. If Locke began with political life, and specifically with *conflict* as the primary fact of existence, he might very well have felt himself obliged to find the source of that conflict in the nature of the individual. In other words, had Locke begun with the individual, he might have concluded that man is essentially sociable, since he is sociable in his most primary existence; instead, Locke may have proceeded from the realm of political conflict to the individual (and even allowed this process to color his conception of all other social relations, *including* family life.)

To begin the discussion of the role of Locke's state of nature, here is one recent commentator's account of the state of nature as a moral construct, which is to be distinguished from man's historical or actual state:

> The state of nature "governed" by the Law of Nature is the only acceptable moral description of man regardless of whether or not, in any particular instance, he succeeds in living in perfect obedience to the commands of that law. "Men living together according to reason, without a common superior on earth with authority to judge between them, is *properly* the state of nature" [quotation from Locke, *Second Treatise*, art. 19].
>   . . . When Locke makes reference to these qualities in his discussion of the state of nature, he does so in the context of qualifying language which reveals that he is speaking of what conditions *would* be like if men lived "according to the law of nature"—because it is *under* that law that "all men alike are friends of one another and are bound together by common interests." [*Essays on the Law of Nature*, Essay V.] Locke is offering us a definitional statement characterizing the law "whereby" men are "united into one fellowship and society." [*Second Treatise*, arts. 128, 172.] His supposed description of the peaceful state of nature refers not to the *state* but to the *law* of nature, to that which ought to exist, according to God's will.[27]

And later in the same article:

> Thus, men are "equipped" with the "faculties" for reasoning. Every man is born "with a *title* to perfect freedom." [*Second Treatise*, art. 87.] It is in this sense that all men are by nature rational and free, in that they possess the capacity to be so. "Thus we are born free as we are born rational, not that we have actually the exercise of either." [*Ibid.*, art. 61.] Similarly, Locke speaks of men as "beings *capable* of laws." And a few sentences later, he asks, "is a man under the law of nature?" His reply is that men in the state of nature are under the law because they are "supposed *capable* to know that law." Not that the individual actually does know it in every instance, but only that "he is *presumed* to know how far that law is to be his guide." [*Ibid.*, arts. 57, 59, 60.][28]

27 Richard Ashcraft, "Locke's State of Nature: Historical Fact or Moral Fiction?" *American Political Science Review*, LXII (September 1968), 906.
28 *Ibid.*, p. 908.

What, then, is the actual state of nature like? This question is most often approached by means of a comparison between Locke and Hobbes. It is possible, of course, simply to judge Locke's ideal state of nature against the "actual" state of Hobbes —as many commentators seem to do, and as Locke himself sometimes apparently does—in which case the contrast is striking.[29] Others, however, have argued that the difference is still fundamental, even if one recognizes the distinction between the moral and the "historical" states of nature in Locke's doctrine. The arguments opposing Locke to Hobbes tend to center on two essential points: (1) that, whatever conflicts may exist in the actual state of nature, the state of war is not a universal condition for Locke, as it is for Hobbes; and (2) that, as Ashcraft argues, Locke's actual state of nature presupposes the possibility, if not the actuality, of man's obedience to moral law, that the law of nature and the actual state of nature are not necessarily mutually exclusive; while for Hobbes, the state of nature is presumably characterized precisely by the impossibility of obedience to moral law and conformity to the law of nature.

The present argument does not rest on a comparison between Hobbes and Locke; but it might be worthwhile, without making too much of the similarities between them, to place their differences in perspective in order to clear the air for the subsequent discussion of Locke's "individualistic" state of nature and its role.

With reference to the first argument just cited, it must be said, to begin with, that in distinguishing between the state of nature and the state of war, which for Hobbes are the same, Locke is probably more interested in dissociating himself from Hobbes's conception of *civil society* than from his portrait of the state of nature and the conception of man it represents. Locke seems concerned to show that, by eliminating the state of war and achieving peace through the establishment of the sovereign

[29] It might be less unfair to compare Locke's ideal state of nature to Hobbes's *law* of nature.

power, Hobbes has not, in fact, effected a transition from the state of nature to civil society, but has at best only established what for Locke would be simply a peaceful state of nature.[30] Hobbes' civil society is for Locke not a genuine civil society at all, since it still fails to meet the latter's criteria of legitimacy. The Hobbesian sovereign may succeed in resolving conflict, but, especially if the sovereign power resides in a single man who is himself above the law, he cannot be regarded as the "impartial judge" whose existence characterizes the civil state for Locke. One *need* not conclude, then, that Locke's argument about the state of nature constitutes a rejection of the Hobbesian conception of man and social relations.

If, however, Locke *is* understood to be addressing himself to Hobbes's state of nature as an expression of the nature of man and social relations, it would seem that he succeeds in setting himself apart from Hobbes only by misrepresenting him. Indeed, the very arguments that Locke uses to distinguish his state of nature from what is presumably a Hobbesian state of war—when he is not actually contrasting the state of war to his own *ideal* state—only serve to reveal certain similarities between Locke's actual state and the Hobbesian one. Locke's account of the state of war very simply refers to the existence of violence and open hostilities: "Want of a Common Judge with Authority puts all men in a State of Nature: Force without Right, upon a Man's Person, makes a State of War. . . ."[31] To deny, then, that the state of war is a universal condition is simply to deny that there is universal and constant physical violence among men. The point, however, is that Hobbes explicitly points out that "the nature of War, consisteth not in actual fighting."[32] Instead, a state of war exists where there is likelihood of open hostilities *"during all the time there is no assurance to the con-*

30 See Ashcraft, *op. cit.*, where this suggestion is discussed in greater detail.
31 Locke, *Second Treatise*, p. 321 (art. 19).
32 Hobbes, *Leviathan*, p. 96 (chap. 13).
33 *Ibid.*

trary." [33] In other words, the state of nature is a state of war insofar as, where no legal sanctions exist to provide some "assurance to the contrary," conflicts are always likely to degenerate into "actual fighting." Interestingly enough, Locke, too, defines his actual state of nature in terms of the likelihood, in the absence of any legal assurances to the contrary, that conflicts will end in open violence:

> To avoid this State of War (wherein there is no appeal but to Heaven, and *wherein every the least difference is apt to end,* where there is no Authority to decide between the contenders) is one great *reason of Mens putting themselves into Society* and quitting the State of Nature.[34]

The theme of uncertainty that plays such an important role in these conceptions of the state of nature is central to the second argument as well. The argument opposing Locke to Hobbes on the grounds that obedience to moral law in the state of nature is conceived as possible by the former but not by the latter, again, somewhat misrepresents Hobbes's position. Without asking how hypothetical or theoretical the "possibility" of obedience to natural law may be even in Locke's case, one might point out that it is not at all clear that Hobbes is arguing against the possibility of obedience to moral law in the state of nature. Rather, he suggests that in the state of nature, since each man must be his own judge, if a man has any reasonable doubt about another's intentions, he is absolved of obligation to the latter. On the other hand, in the civil state such doubt does not constitute sufficient grounds for breach of obligation, since there is an external authority to compel the other to "perform" his contract, however doubtful the latter's intentions may be. Wherever there is trust, there is obligation; but in the state of nature, trust can be based only on individual judgment, with no external assurances. The following quotation clearly indicates that Hobbes is able to conceive of trust and obligation to contracts

[34] Locke, *Second Treatise,* p. 323 (art. 21). Emphasis of the phrase, "wherein ... end," added.

in the state of nature, even if the conditions of obligation are different from those under a civil authority:

> If a Covenant be made, wherein neither of the parties performe presently, but trust one another; in the condition of meer Nature, (which is a condition of Warre of every man against every man), upon any reasonable suspition, it is Voyd: But if there be a common Power set over them both, with right and force sufficient to compell performance; it is not Voyd.[35]

It may also be worth commenting that the very appearance of the famous phrase, "Warre of every man against every man," in a passage that indicates the possibility of trust and obedience to obligation in the state of nature, suggests that the Hobbesian concepts of "war" and the state of nature have a meaning somewhat different from the one often attributed to them.

Nevertheless, whatever the similarities or differences between Hobbes and Locke, there is a more fundamental sense in which Locke's actual state of nature embodies "individualistic" and antagonistic human relationships, in sharp contrast to the communitarian, fraternal relationships symbolized by the moral state of nature and replacing, or at least profundly modifying, the latter as the "only acceptable moral description of man." In the final analysis, Locke's civil society is *not* morally based on a state of nature that corresponds to the law of nature whereby men are "friends," equal and united in "common interests." Instead, it is based on *another* state of nature, characterized by property and class relations, extreme inequalities, and consequent antagonisms and conflicting interests—a state that is legitimized and given moral status by *consent*.

As C. B. Macpherson has shown, Locke's position can be understood by considering the pivotal role that the invention of money plays in his account of the historical state of nature.[36]

---

35 Hobbes, *op. cit.*, p. 105 (chap. 14).
36 C. B. Macpherson, *op. cit.* Macpherson has been criticized for arguing that Locke in the end gives inequality the status of natural law, for attributing too much significance to money as a removal of the natural-law limitation on the acquisition of property, for ascribing to Locke a commit-

The primary significance of the invention of money for Locke is not simply that it affects the natural limitation on property acquisition, but rather that, insofar as money provides a means of establishing gross property differentials greater than could be accounted for by differences in industriousness alone, consent to money means consent to such differentials. Locke takes great pains to point out that consent to money represents consent to its consequences:

> . . . it is plain, that Men have agreed to disproportionate and un-equal Possession of the Earth, they having by a tacit and voluntary consent found out a way, how a man may fairly possess more land than he himself can use the product of. . . .[37]

Locke has, by interpreting the invention of money as consent to its consequences, found a way of justifying those consequences —property and class differentials and all that goes with them— and making them a limiting condition on civil society with a contractual, moral priority over civil society. In other words, natural law is not the only condition that has such priority. Even without somehow "altering" natural law, Locke can add further limitations on civil society by establishing a prior agreement. The invention of money occurs in the state of nature, that is, prior to civil society. Surely, any subsequent agreement is bound by the conditions of a prior agreement, if the latter has not been abrogated.

Thus, the difference between the nonmonetary and monetary states of nature, whether or not it corresponds to the distinction between the actual and the ideal, is extremely significant: the latter state is characterized by significant inequalities and their attendant consequences. Moreover, the consequences of these

---

ment to unlimited acquisition and a moral attachment to the acquisitive spirit as such. No matter how justified these criticisms may be, it can be said that none of these points need be accepted to accept the significance of Macpherson's argument. Certainly, the following discussion does not depend on any of these controversial suggestions.

37 Locke, *Second Treatise*, p. 365 (art. 50)

inequalities, as we shall see, are quite significant and far-reaching for Locke, sufficiently so that one is justified in regarding them as the basis of a class system.[38] The crucial point is that civil society arises out of, and is based upon, this monetary state, presupposing man's consent to, and therefore the justice of, such a system. Therefore, this system is a given, a limiting factor, an initial premise of civil society; and everything that Locke says about civil society must be considered in this light. In a sense, one fundamental purpose of civil society is to protect and enforce this prior agreement to inequality; and the purpose of a contract establishes the conditions of obligation to it. Moreover, as long as money exists, the conditions it represents are legitimate and binding.

To return finally to Polin's argument, then, when Locke says that man is fundamentally a social being, the statement is, on the one hand, simply a prescription—a prescription, moreover, that is superseded or severely qualified by another quite contrary norm. On the other hand, if one takes the statement as empirical, one is left with little more than an externalized "sociability" based on egoistic prudence, material need, and a desire for security. This sociable prudence is supported by contracts guaranteed by coercive power, and a proper system of education ultimately resting on sovereign power and on a religion of reward and punishment.[39] In the final analysis, sociability depends very heavily on the fear of coercive sanctions, imposed either by the sovereign or by God, and not on any association, or even compatibility, with individuality in the human psyche.

Nevertheless, one might still want to speak of Locke's concept

38 Locke's liberal successors abandon the concept of a state of nature, but not the psychology of individualism or the kind of social relationships that arise out of it. Thus, in a sense, for these later thinkers the relationship between that psychology and political prescriptions, which Locke establishes somewhat indirectly, becomes more immediate.

39 See especially Hobbes, *Leviathan*, chaps. 12 and 30; and Locke, *Essay*, I, 474–75 (Bk. II, chap. xxviii, arts. 5–8); and the whole of Locke's *Reasonableness of Christianity*, with its discussion of Christianity as an important force in socializing the masses.

of society as reflecting, in one sense, a "natural" sociability and perhaps even a unity of individuality and sociality, insofar as he has a notion of *society* as distinct from political order. Some commentators—notably Sheldon Wolin in his *Politics and Vision* [40]—emphasize the importance for Locke's thought of his "discovery" of society as a self-subsistent entity, as a principle of spontaneous cohesion prior to and independent of political arrangements. This would suggest that some form of society exists prior to civil society and it would follow that within civil society there is some principle of cohesion independent of political coercion. Assuming, then, that one can speak of certain social relations as "natural" in Locke's theory, the important question is the particular character of those natural social relations and what they imply about the relationship between individuality and sociality. In this connection, it might be worthwhile to recall the previous suggestion, supported by C. B. Macpherson's argument, that Locke simply abstracts his idea of the state of nature from society as it exists in his own day, and that he seeks to justify that society as natural by placing its prototype in the state of nature.

What this means is that the social relations that Locke regards as natural are the relations of property, class, and the network of interacting interests that characterize his perception of the existing—and the ideal—society. Wolin's account of Locke's concept of society is quite compatible with this interpretation. The attribution of such a concept of natural society to Locke is extremely significant in light of the arguments being proposed in this essay.

To begin with, it should be noted that the idea of a "natural" society in the above-mentioned sense is not incompatible with the idea of a society based on contract. For the most part, the concept of a social contract is a metaphorical way of saying something about the nature of obligation, for example, or about

[40] Sheldon Wolin, *Politics and Vision* (Boston: Little, Brown and Co., 1960), esp. pp. 286 ff.

the nature of the social relations that prevail, or ought to prevail, in a particular kind of human society. As an example of the use of the "contract" idea in a general sense as a metaphor about the nature of existing social relations, one might refer to the distinction many sociologists have made between *Gemeinschaft* and *Gesellschaft* as two different principles of human association. The former is characterized essentially by affective or familial relations; the latter, by "contractual" or largely externalized functional relations, what might be called relations of *utility*. A modern commercial or industrial society, insofar as its social relations are based on specialization and division of labor, market relations, etc., would be said to be characterized by contractual relations. From this point of view, if one regards Locke's "natural society" as one based essentially on property and class relations and the interaction of interests—as Macpherson does and as Wolin in a somewhat more complex way seems to—it is still possible to speak of that society as a network of contractual relations, a society based on contract, utility, the coercion of material want, and so on—as this essay has done up to now. To say, however, that Locke conceives of such a natural human society as yet tells us nothing about our main concern, about the relationship between man's selfhood and his sense of community, or the relationship between his individuality and his sociality.

At this point, something should be said about the sense in which it *might* be argued that individuality and sociality are united in Locke's concept of the natural society. As has been pointed out earlier, the idea is expressed rather nicely by Bernard Mandeville's formula "Private vices, publick benefits," which in one form or another was to become quite popular in liberal thought. A similar idea is reflected in Alexander Pope's couplet in the "Essay on Man": "Thus God and Nature link'd the general frame, And bade Self-love and Social be the same." Again, the same principle is elaborated in a complex and sophisticated way in Adam Smith's ideas on the harmony of selfish interests operating through the market mechanism. The market, as Smith conceives of it, provides the perfect model for the society based on egoism, in which egoism itself becomes a principle of cohesion. In other words, the market society in a sense unites individuality and sociality, but only insofar as individuality is equated with egoism. The man whose individuality is expressed in terms of egoism—more specifically, acquisitive and possessive egoism—is also sociable in the utilitarian sense that his interests drive him into relations of division of labor, exchange, and so on. While Locke's purely economic ideas have not quite advanced to the point of Smith's market economics, one can perhaps regard his *political* theory as a precursor of Smith's economics. The egoism of Locke's man is perhaps more immediately linked with sociality than is that of Hobbesian man, because in the latter egoism seems to lead to sociality via the prudential establishment of civil society, while in the former egoism relies somewhat less on civil society and establishes directly a more cohesive network of utilitarian or "contractual" social relations independent of political order.[41]

Nevertheless, the union of egoism and community contains an inherent contradiction, an antagonism that ultimately cannot be resolved. Egoism is already by definition a denial of the community. Insofar as individuality, as egoism, compels man to submit to the community, that individuality is in a very fundamental sense self-contradictory, self-annihilating. This is true in several ways. It should be noted, to begin with, that the equation between "private vices" and "public benefits" is not perfect. In the final analysis, additional factors must be introduced to balance the equation. It is significant, for example, that liberalism *is not* anarchism. The "invisible hand" is, after all, generally assisted by the coercive force of government. Government is necessary precisely because individual wills cannot be expected to

---

41 Of course, it is, again, not entirely accurate to speak of Hobbes's state of nature as nonsocial, but it seems clear that Hobbes chooses to emphasize the degree to which society is dependent upon political arrangements.

converge in a truly public expression. This is important because the consequence is that government must, in effect, represent the public being of citizens who are essentially private. In so doing, it trespasses on human autonomy and individuality—and ironically on egoism itself—or, to put it another way, it "dismembers" man by separating his public from his private being: this point will be discussed further in the final chapter below. The liberal view here outlined will be contrasted with, for example, Rousseau's concept of the general will, which expresses precisely the possibility of convergence in all men of public and private, to a sufficient extent that their public beings need not be represented by a force alien to them.[42]

Even leaving aside the question of government, however, and paying due respect to the liberal fear of political tyranny, it can be said that the philosophers of egoism rely, in the absence of *political* tyranny, on what has been called the "tyranny of society," the pressure for conformity—i.e. the suppression of individuality—to insure that private vices will, in fact, give rise to public benefits. The pressure for conformity is another way in which society can make socially acceptable behavior a necessity for egoism, so that, paradoxically, egoism, which is the expression of individuality, again becomes the enemy of individuality, and even the demands of egoism work against egoism.[43]

Ironically, J. S. Mill, always regarded as liberalism's most ardent defender of individuality and diversity, also provides the most explicit statement on the importance of conformity in liberal society. He makes it clear that, precisely because men are egoistic and because relations in society tend to be antagonistic, conformity becomes the very essence of the social bond:

Further, as the strongest propensities of human nature (being the

---

42 This problem too, as we shall see more clearly in the final chapter, can be regarded as a dimension of the subject-object question—the question of the separation or reunification of subject and object, and the autonomy or heteronomy of the subject and the self.
43 See Wolin, *op. cit.*, pp. 343–51, for a discussion of the importance of conformity in liberal thought.

purely selfish ones and those of a sympathetic character which partake most of the nature of selfishness) evidently tend in themselves to disunite mankind, not to unite them—to make them rivals, not confederates—social existence is only possible by a disciplining of those more powerful propensities, which consists in subordinating them to a common system of opinions. The degree of this subordination is the measure of the completeness of the social union, and the nature of the common opinions determines its kind.[44]

Thus, even the view that individuality, in the form of egoism, gives rise to a "natural" society nevertheless still implies a basic and irreconcilable antagonism between individuality and sociality. There is, however, an even more fundamental sense in which the view of society here outlined is different from the "dialectical" view and inimical to individuality in a broader sense. The essential difference is, to put it simply, that the "Lockean" concept of society treats men as objects, while the "dialectical" concept treats men as subjects—both in keeping with their respective treatments of the subject-object relation. If the dialectical view of human community can be referred to

44 John Stuart Mill, *A System of Logic* (London: Longmans, Green and Co., 1967), p. 605 (Bk. VI, chap. x, art. 7). Mill's comments are particularly significant when one considers that he is usually credited with greater insight into the dangers of social pressures for conformity than are any of his liberal predecessors. Moreover, it is not at all clear that this statement on the social function of conformity actually contradicts the doctrine of individuality expressed in "On Liberty." A careful examination of that work reveals that, despite the insight into social pressure attributed to him, ultimately Mill is really concerned about social pressures that are politically enforced; and that he has, at best, a rather inadequate appreciation of more subtle pressures and, in fact, *advocates* a considerable degree of social compulsion. Even more important (and perhaps this interpretation would make "On Liberty" not quite as incongruous with the rest of his philosophy as was suggested earlier, at least with respect to the majority of men), it seems that his whole argument rests on the conviction that the masses of men will conform in any case, and, indeed, that this is as it should be, since mass conformity is the condition for social order. The defense of individuality is clearly and explicitly meant to protect an élite few, and need not be understood as a rejection of the principle suggested in the *System of Logic*. Similar assumptions about the role of mass conformity seem to be operative, at least implicitly, in other liberal theories as well; again, Locke's *Reasonableness of Christianity* would seem to suggest much the same view.

as "intersubjectivity," perhaps we can call the Lockean community "interobjectivity."

This rather precious language, of course, needs to be explained. Very simply, what is meant is that certain concepts of society—such as, for example, those based on the market model or property relations—tend to emphasize, more than the interaction of men, the interaction of objective forces, the interaction of interests, of functions, of roles, and of men only insofar as they are *possessors* or *occupants* of interests, functions, or roles. Society is a network of interacting interests and roles, and men are defined in terms of those interests and roles. Even human freedom consists, to quote Marx, in "the right to the undisturbed enjoyment of accidents of fortune," [45] the accidents of class, the laws of the market, and so on. In its most extreme form—and, of course, Locke himself does not carry it nearly so far, although Bentham comes closer, and certain modern social scientists even more so—such a concept of society seems almost to suggest that men are simply points at which several roles or functions intersect.

The central place given to the concept of *interest* in liberal thought is particularly illuminating in this connection. The idea that human activity can ultimately be defined in terms of interest contributed significantly to the conception of man as an "externalized" creature, an *object*. Interest in effect replaced man's inner being; and man became simply the reflexive creature of external, largely material objects which attracted or repelled him, his relation to those objects, of course, being to a great extent determined by his class and economic position. Man became, in essence, a receptacle for interests.

The particular "objectified" form that the concept of interest takes in liberal philosophy can perhaps be explained by its association with empiricist psychology. "Interest" is simply a

45 Karl Marx, *German Ideology*, in *Writings of the Young Marx on Philosophy and Sociology*, trans. and ed. L. D. Easton and K. H. Guddat (Garden City, N.Y.: Anchor Books, Doubleday and Co., 1967), p. 460.

generalized expression of human motives and passions, attractions and repulsions; and as such, it would certainly follow the rules that empiricist psychology ascribes to specific motives and passions. The important point is that a psychology for which the only "objects" for man are the objects given in sense experience (reason, for example, constitutes no objects), and action is determined by pleasures and pains (or "uneasinesses") arising out of such impressions, finds it rather difficult to account for anything else but the most tangible, even material, objects, acting very directly on man, as the causes of human response and the sources of motives to action. Moreover, the empiricist view tends for this same reason to regard men as, so to speak, reflexes of such external, material objects. Although this outlook may be more easily associated with the psychology of Hume—when he remains true to it—and with his utilitarian successors, it can be argued, as Hume himself would argue, that it is already implicit in Locke's doctrine, inasmuch as Locke also denies the existence of objects not given in sense experience and confines the role of reason to ordering sense impressions and extracting from them implications that are already given in the object. Moreover, Locke, too, cannot consistently admit any human motives other than "uneasinesses" deriving from sense impressions.

Particularly if this concept of interest is considered in the light of a view (like that of Locke cited above in chap. 2, n. 38) according to which men experience each other only in the most externalized way, it is not difficult to see how the interaction of objectified interests becomes the principle of an "interobjective" form of community. Perhaps our contrast between two concepts of community can, then, be crystallized into a distinction between *interest* and *compassion* as two principles of community—the one, an objective principle the force of which is external to man; the other, a subjective impulse generated by the inner self.

Wolin discusses interest and its relationship to the process of objectification in liberal thought, for example, in connection with Bentham's substitution of *interest* for conscience and, in general, for the human "soul":

> The epitaph for conscience was stated by Bentham in his usual bald way when he said it was "a thing of fictitious existence." And Bentham also made it abundantly clear that men no longer had any real incentive to that self-knowledge which leads to the examination of the inner life.
>
> "But by interest he is at the same time diverted from any close examination into the springs by which his own conduct is determined. From such knowledge he has not, in any ordinary shape, any thing to gain,—he finds not in it any source of enjoyment."
>
> At the same time, since every act of will and of the intellect was reducible to interest, there remained nothing to examine internally: man's soul had been factored out.
>
> Having reduced man to mere externality and stripped him of conscience, it was easy for the liberal economists to treat him as a material object—a style of analysis which later provoked the bitter denunciation of Marx.[46]

The process of reduction, externalization, and objectification goes so far that a classical economist is able, for example, to speak of the laborer this way:

> A laborer is himself a portion of the national capital; and is to be considered in all investigations of this sort, merely as a machine which it has required a certain quantity of labor to construct. . . .[47]

It seems clear that Locke does not objectify man to the extent that Bentham does; nevertheless, even for Locke, man is to a very considerable degree defined in terms of his objective status or role. One need only consider the place of property and class in Locke's doctrine. To begin with, Locke's theory of property itself embodies the definition of freedom as compatible with subjection to external objective—in this case, social—conditions and forces. An essential component of Locke's doctrine—and of

46 Wolin, *op. cit.*, p. 341.
47 *Ibid.*, p. 342.

all subsequent liberal doctrines of liberty—is the principle of *freedom of contract*. The way in which this principle is conceived is an extremely revealing key to the liberal conception of freedom. Significantly, for Locke, as for all liberals until T. H. Green (one of whose central concerns was a rejection of this liberal conception of free contract), there is no contradiction between, on the one hand, the notion of a free contract and, on the other, the acceptance of gross inequality between the contractors, which makes the "voluntary" act of one party virtually a necessity. According to this conception of a free contract, freedom is considered to be unaffected by the unequal constraints and the subordination of one man to another that are necessarily imposed on men by the realities of their social and economic status, by property and class differentials. Again, not only is such a conception of freedom not foreign to Locke, but, indeed, it is central to his theory of property. This conception of free contract provides the justification for wage labor, which might otherwise seem incompatible with Locke's association of labor and property, and establishes the *right*—a right which is essential to Locke's doctrine—of one man to property acquired by means of another man's labor. It is not unreasonable to suggest, then, that this conception of freedom of contract makes the particular nature of any man's right to property—and even to his person, since labor and property are extensions of his person—vary with his status and the particular meaning and role which that status attaches to his labor.

This determination of man's being by his social condition, by "accidents of fortune," is further reflected in the role played by *class* in Locke's doctrine. It has already been suggested that Locke finds a way of legitimizing profound inequalities not grounded in nature, and that these inequalities are so pervasive and far-reaching in their consequences that it is possible to speak of Locke's social theory as presupposing and justifying a class system. Although he begins with the principle of the natural equality of men, he ends by accepting—even basing his entire system upon—inequalities arising, according to his own argument, from nonnatural class differentials. Moreover, these inequalities are expressed in characteristics as basic to the essence of man as rationality and the capacity for morality. In the end, Locke in an important sense abandons the doctrine of equality altogether and speaks of the inequalities in rationality and morality, which he seems at first to have attributed to property differentials, as if they were divinely ordained and as if they justified the perpetuation of social inequalities. Man's very essence is, then, determined by his social status.

Any attempt to determine the precise nature of the relationship between rationality and property in Locke encounters Locke's own ambivalence concerning which is prior: inequality in initial rationality or inequality in property. Do some men acquire more property because they are inherently more rational, or do they become more rational because they have somehow acquired more property? In a sense, however, the question is unimportant.

The point is precisely that the initial, natural status of men becomes irrelevant as a consequence of subsequent property differentials. Locke makes it quite clear that it is members of the propertied class who have the opportunity to develop their rationality and morality. Their preeminence is thus justified and, for all practical purposes, self-perpetuating. In other words, despite Locke's professions concerning the natural moral equality of men, he is quite prepared to base a system of social and political inequality on the presumed moral inequalities that may have arisen out of "accidents of fortune"—economic inequalities.

To support this view, one might cite in particular Locke's discussion of morality in *The Reasonableness of Christianity.* Here Locke is clearly distinguishing between two kinds of morality: one based on reason (and faith), the other on faith and obedience alone—what one might call the morality of leaders and that of followers. Moreover, he tends to associate each kind of morality with a class: the higher with the propertied, the other with laborers, tradesmen, etc. One of his most often repeated themes, in this work and elsewhere (e.g. in his economic works), is the "lack of leisure and education" among the "multitude"—the latter being explicitly equated with the nonpropertied classes—which on the whole makes them incapable of achieving a higher level of rationality: ". . . the labourer's share, being seldom more than a bare subsistence, never allows that body of men, time, or opportunity to raise their thoughts above that. . . ."[48] They are capable of morality, yes, but it is the morality of obedience, not of reason:

> The greatest part of mankind want leisure or capacity for demonstration. . . . And you may as soon hope to have all the day-labourers and tradesmen, the spinsters and dairy-maids, perfect mathematicians, as to have them perfect in ethics this way. Hearing plain commands, is the sure and only course to bring them to obedience and practice. The greatest part cannot know, and therefore they must believe.[49]

This impression is strengthened by Locke's work on education, which seems designed to perpetuate this condition of moral inequality by suggesting, in effect, different forms of education according to the "calling" of one's class, or even for the leaders and the led (or perhaps none at all for the latter):

> The well educating of their children is so much the duty and concern of parents, and the welfare and prosperity of the nation so much depends on it, that I would have every one lay it seriously to heart; and . . . set his helping hand to promote every where that way of training up youth, with regard to their several conditions, which is the easiest, shortest, and likeliest to produce virtuous, useful, and able men in their distinct callings: though that most to be taken care of, is the gentleman's calling. For if those of that rank are by their education once set right, they will quickly bring all the rest into order.[50]

48 Locke, *Some Considerations of the Lowering of Interest*, in *Works*, 9th ed. (London: Longmans *et al.*, 1794), IV, 71.
49 Locke, *The Reasonableness of Christianity*, in *Works*, IX, 146.
50 Locke, *Some Thoughts Concerning Education*, in *Works*, VIII, v.

In short, it would seem that religion for the lower classes serves the purpose of teaching them to obey; education for the lower classes serves the purpose of teaching them to follow. The propertied classes are educated for leadership, to rule, to guide, to govern.[51] Apparently, they have the right to rule on the basis of the access to higher rationality and morality that their station gives them. Thus, of course, the system tends to be self-perpetuating.

To return, then, to our earlier argument about money in Locke's theory, the consequences that have been consented to through the invention of money are quite significant ones. For example, if inequality of possessions, no matter how it originates, tends to give rise to inequality in rationality, etc., and hence in qualifications for political power, consent to property inequalities in effect means consent to the existence of a ruling class. All these consequences, moreover, are prior to civil society, which embodies and institutionalizes them, having been in a sense established to enforce them.

Adam Smith provides a more explicit and consistent—and perhaps less disingenuous—statement of some of these Lockean principles:

The difference of natural talents in different men is in reality, much less than we are aware of; and the very different genius which appears to distinguish men of different professions, when grown up to maturity, is not upon many occasions so much the cause, as the ef-

---

[51] The following statement is sometimes cited as evidence that Locke restricts even representation to the propertied classes: ". . . the number of members, in all places, that have a right to be distinctly represented, which no part of the People however incorporated can pretend to, but in a proportion to the assistance, which it affords to the publick . . ." (*Second Treatise*, art. 158).

It may also be worth introducing an interesting historical note. At least in law property qualification for membership in Parliament did *not* exist in the seventeenth century, although in *1696* a bill establishing such a qualification passed both Houses. (The king refused to consent, so that a successful bill was not introduced until 1710.) In other words, it was the new Parliament under the leadership of the Whig—Somers—faction that attempted to have this qualification introduced. These were Locke's closest political friends, acting at the time of Locke's greatest political success and influence.

fect of the division of labor. The difference between the most dissimilar characters, between a philosopher and a common street porter, for example, seems to arise not so much from nature, as from habit, custom, and education. When they came into the world, and for the first six or eight years of their existence, they were, perhaps, very much alike, and neither their parents nor playfellows could perceive any remarkable difference. About that age, or soon after, they came to be employed in very different occupations. The difference of talents comes then to be taken notice of, and widens by degrees, till at last the vanity of the philosopher is willing to acknowledge scarce any resemblance. But without the disposition to truck, barter, and exchange, every necessity and convenience of life which he wanted, all must have had the same duties to perform, and the same work to do and there could have been no such difference of employment as could alone give occasion to any great difference of talents.

As it is this disposition which forms that difference of talents, so remarkable among men of different professions, so it is this same disposition which renders that difference useful.[52]

Man's individuality, then, is a function of his role, and this is all to the good; for that is how society's work gets done. In fact, that is how society is bound together. Moreover, freedom is the free play of objective economic forces, and human liberty lies in the individual's right to enjoy relatively undisturbed the "accidents of fortune" arising from that free play of market forces. Perhaps it is unreasonable at this stage in the history of economic thought to expect from Smith any other solution, or even a more humane attitude with regard to the one he describes; but one cannot help being struck by the complacency and even moral approval with which he is prepared to accept the contradiction inherent in his views on equality.

In this connection, it is illuminating to compare Locke's

---

52 Adam Smith, *The Wealth of Nations*, ed. E. Cannan (New York: Modern Library, 1937), pp. 15–16. One might add that, while later liberalism is certainly more democratic than Locke and perhaps more "humane" than Smith, the contradiction between convictions about natural equality and the acceptance of substantial social inequalities persists, as does the tendency, though somewhat modified by welfare-state ideas, to define human liberty in terms of "accidents of fortune."

theory of education with that of Rousseau, who, as we have seen, can be regarded as an exponent of the view that treats man as "subject." Here, in a matter so central to the development of the individual, Locke is perhaps more explicit than usual about the degree to which man's very being is to be determined by his role, his station in life. As we have seen, each child is, quite simply, to be educated differently from the outset to fit his particular station, his calling—and by "calling" Locke means not only an individual's profession, but the special role assigned by society to his class. Thus, Locke's remarks on education are, by his own testimony, appropriate only to the "gentleman's calling," and nothing else. Moreover, it may even be unnecessary for the lower classes to be educated at all, provided that their benevolent guardians, the "gentlemen" whose calling it is to lead and rule, are properly educated. Again, Locke begins even in this work with statements about the natural equality of men and about the infinite malleability of the human mind, and ends with a program of education based on, and designed to perpetuate, social inequalities deriving, not from nature, but from "accidents of fortune."

Compare Locke's remarks, cited above, to the following passage from Rousseau:

> . . . where social ranks alone remain fixed, while the men who form them are constantly changing, no one knows whether he is not working against his son by educating him for his own rank.
>
> In the natural order men are all equal and their common calling is that of manhood and whoever is well educated for that calling cannot do badly in those related to it. It hardly matters to me whether my pupil is destined for the army, the church, or the law. Before his parents chose a calling for him, nature called him to the life of a man. Life is the trade I want to teach him. When he leaves my hands, I grant you, he will be neither a magistrate, a soldier, nor a priest; he will be above all a man. . . .[53]

---

[53] Rousseau, *Emile, op. cit.,* IV, 251–52: ". . . ou les rangs seuls demeurent, et ou les hommes en changent sans cesse, nul ne sait si en élevant son fils pour le sien il ne travaille pas contre lui.

"Dans l'ordre naturel les hommes étant tous égaux leur vocation commune

Rousseau is, in effect, educating man to transcend "accidents of fortune." He is educating man in a sense as self-active subject, rather than as the passive function of objective forces who is to be made to fit his proper objective role. This conception of education reflects Rousseau's social views as a whole. In his *Social Contract* he is quite simply seeking a principle of society based on a community of men, not a network of roles. In a very important sense, this is the object of his emphasis on equality. A substantial degree of social equality minimizes the extent to which men are identified in terms of their social status or roles. Moreover, equality minimizes the antagonism between individual and community by allowing men to express their individuality in forms other than envious and competitive egoism.

In short, Rousseau is seeking a principle of political society based on a different relationship between individual and community than that implicit in the Lockean view. Life in society need not, for Rousseau, weaken individuality, first, because his society does not define man in terms of his status or role. More-

---

est l'état d'homme, et quiconque est bien élevé pour celui-là ne peut mal remplir ceux qui s'y rapportent. Qu'on destine mon élève à l'épée, à l'église, au barreau, peu m'importe. Avant la vocation des parents la nature l'appelle à la vie humaine. Vivre est le métier que je lui veux apprendre. En sortant de mes mains il ne sera, j'en conviens, ni magistrat, ni soldat, ni prêtre: il sera prémièrement homme. . . ."

This can certainly be regarded as one of the more revolutionary of Rousseau's ideas. To quote Hannah Arendt in her discussion of the American Founding Fathers: ". . . no revolutionary ever thought it his task to introduce mankind to it [the game of status-seeking] or to teach the underprivileged the rules of the game. How alien these present-day categories would have been to the minds of the founders of the republic can perhaps best be seen in their attitude to the question of education, which was of great importance to them, not, however, in order to enable every citizen to rise on the social ladder, but because the welfare of the country and the functioning of its political institutions hinged upon education of all citizens. They demanded 'that every citizen should receive an education proportioned to the condition and pursuits of his life,' whereby it was understood that for the purpose of education the citizens would 'be divided into two classes—the laboring and the learned'. . . ." [the quotations coming from one of the more democratic of the revolutionaries, Thomas Jefferson]: Hannah Arendt, *On Revolution* (New York: The Viking Press, 1965), p. 67.

over, unlike the liberals, Rousseau can envisage a situation in which community is a function of individual consciousness, generated by the self rather than imposed from without by social, political, or material coercion. A free political society is one in which the people represent themselves and their own "public being." Insofar as man lives in society, only a self-generated principle of community, only a situation in which individuality and community can be united in consciousness, is compatible with individual autonomy.[54] Moreover, a society that is not fragmented and atomized by an inherent antagonism between man and man need not impose order by demanding conformity, since diversity is disruptive only when it is super-imposed upon more fundamental conflicts and antagonisms.

Like Mill, Rousseau sees conformity as a necessary force to preserve order in a fundamentally antagonistic society. Since for Rousseau, however, such a society is not an inevitable consequence of man's nature, but rather a sign of corruption, conformity does not represent the ultimate principle of social unity, but instead reflects a breakdown of the social bond. Conformity is part of the deceptive veil that obscures a situation in which society is so structured that men are necessarily enemies, because their interests are necessarily antagonistic—a situation in which "every man finds his profit in the misfortunes of his neighbor" and, because men must be enemies, peaceful relations among them can be maintained only by deception:

> Let us penetrate, therefore, beyond frivolous demonstrations of be-
> nevolence to what happens in the depths of the heart, and let us
> reflect what must be the state of things when all men are forced to
> caress and destroy one another at the same time; and when they are
> born enemies by duty, and knaves by interest. If I am told that so-
> ciety is so formed that every man gains by serving others, I shall reply
> that this would be all very well, if he did not gain still more by in-
> juring them . . . Nothing is required but to find a way to insure
> impunity.[55]

54 For more on these points, see below, pp. 161–173.
55 Rousseau, "Discours sur l'origine de l'inégalité," *op. cit.*, III, 203 (Rous-

Conformity helps to create that protective wall of superficial appearances that allows men to act with impunity, so that the underlying antagonisms and mutual destruction do not immediately issue in chaos:

> Today, now that more subtle study and a more refined taste have reduced the art of pleasing to a set of principles, there reigns in modern manners a servile and deceptive uniformity, so that one would think every mind had been cast in the same mould. . . . We no longer dare seem what we really are; and under this perpetual constraint, the herd of men which we call society, when placed in the same circumstances, all act alike, unless very powerful motives prevent them. Thus we never know with whom we have to deal. . . . What a train of vices must accompany this uncertainty! There is no more sincere friendship; no more real esteem; no more deep confidence. Jealousy, suspicion, fear, coldness, reserve, hate, and fraud are constantly concealed under that uniform and deceitful veil of politeness. . . .[56]

To summarize what has been said about theories of sociality in this chapter, then, Rousseau's doctrine has served as an example of the approach to human community which conceives of

---

seau's note IX): "Qu'on pénètre donc au travers de nos frivoles démonstrations de bienveillance ce qui se passe au fond des coeurs, et qu'on refléchisse à ce que doit être un état de choses ou tous les hommes sont forcés de se caresser et de se détruire mutuellement, et ou ils naissent ennemis par devoir et fourbes par intérêt. Si l'on me répond que la Société est tellement constitué que chaque homme gagne à servir les autres; je répliquerai que cela seroit fort bien s'il ne gagnoit encore plus à leur nuire . . . Il ne s'agit donc plus que de trouver les moyens de s'assurer l'impunité. . . ."

[56] Rousseau, "Discours sur les sciences et les arts," in *Oeuvres Complètes,* III, 8 (Part I): "Aujourd'hui que des recherches plus subtiles et un gout plus fine ont réduit l'Art de plaire en principes, il règne dans nos moeurs une vile et trompeuse uniformité, et tous les esprits semblent avoir été jettés dans un même moule. . . . On n'ose plus paroître ce qu'on est; et dans cette contrainte perpétuelle, les hommes que forment ce troupeau qu'on appelle société, placés dans les mêmes circonstances, feront tous les mêmes choses si des motifs plus puissans ne les en détournent. On ne saura donc jamais bien à qui l'on a affaire. . . .

"Quel cortége di vice n'accompagnera point cette incertitude? Plus d'amitiés sinceres; plus d'estime réelle; plus de confiance fondée. Les soupçons, les ombrages, les craintes, la froide, la reserve, la haine, la trahison se cacheront sans cesse sous ce voile uniforme et perfide de politesse. . . ."

sociality as an internal spiritual necessity as fundamental to man's psyche as his individuality, and in fact united with individuality in his consciousness; a conception that can envisage a community through which individuality is strengthened rather than weakened, in which individuality and sociality reinforce each other. This is a conception that is most concisely expressed in Marx's proposition that "Man is in the most literal sense of the word a *zoon politikon,* not only a social animal, but an animal which can develop into an individual only in society."[57] This conception of the relationship between individuality and sociality has been contrasted with the liberal conception, according to which the two are antagonistic and individuality is self-annihilating in the sense that it demands a sociality ultimately inimical to it. In short, this is a conception in which there is an eternal tension inherent in individuality and between individuality and sociality, and neither the one nor the other can ever be fully realized.

The contrast here outlined can be sharpened by concluding this discussion with a brief word about Marx, who himself contrasts the two forms of relationship between individuality and sociality most forcibly by opposing them to each other as two forms of historical reality. Marx in a sense accepts the liberal idea of the relationship; but, like Rousseau, he sees it as the reflection of a particular historical and social situation, an expression of man's *alienation* from himself, not of a universal condition. His object is to reconstruct society in such a way as to overcome that alienation by embodying the unity of individuality and sociality in the structure of society.

Marx's theory of history can be explained—as Jean-Paul Sartre, for example, explains it—in such a way as to illuminate this contrast and reveal its possible implications for our central themes: liberty and community and the relationship between the two. According to this theory, fundamental antagonisms

57 Marx, *A Contribution to the Critique of Political Economy* (Chicago: Charles H. Kerr and Co., 1913), p. 268.

among men, or between individuality and sociality, are the conditions for enslavement to the impersonal forces of history. It is, in fact, to a great extent such antagonisms that make history appear to operate according to immanent laws, independent of human will. Historical and social determinism, human heteronomy, is, then, not a universal, immutable fact but in a very important sense a function of social antagonism. Through community, man can achieve historical autonomy, the "power to make History by pursuing his own ends."[58] Community is the condition for individual liberation from the impersonal forces of history. To quote Sartre:

> ... if History escapes me, this is not because I do not make it; it is because the other is making it as well....
>
> Thus man makes History; this means that he objectifies himself in it and is alienated in it. In this sense History, which is the proper work of *all* activity and of *all* men, appears to men as a foreign force exactly insofar as they do not recognize the meaning of their enterprise ... in the total, objective result.... Marxism in the nineteenth century is a gigantic attempt not only to make History but to get a grip on it, practically and theoretically, by uniting the workers' movement and by clarifying the Proletariat's action through an understanding both of the capitalist process and of the worker's objective reality. At the end of this effort, by the unification of the exploited and by the progressive reduction of the number of classes in the struggle, History was finally to have a meaning for man.[59]

Thus, instead of confronting a situation in which the objective results of their historical acts were necessarily divorced from their individual ends—as the product of conflicting goals must always be something opposed to any one of those goals—men in a sense were to outwit Hegel's "cunning of History" by uniting themselves so that their common goal would actually be reflected in the results of the historical process. In capitalist society, however,

58 Jean-Paul Sartre, *Search for a Method*, trans. Hazel Barnes (New York: Vintage Books, 1968), p. 164.
59 *Ibid.*, p. 89.

Within the unity of his own enterprise, each person surpasses the other and incorporates him as a means (and vice versa); each pair of unifying relations is in turn surpassed by the enterprise of a third. Thus at each level there are constituted hierarchies of enveloping and enveloped ends, where the former steal the significance from the latter and the latter aim at shattering the former. Each time that the enterprise of a man or of a group of men becomes an object for other men who surpass it toward their ends and for the whole of society, this enterprise guards its finality as its real unity, and it becomes, for the very people who initiated it, an external object which tends to dominate and survive them. . . . Thus are constituted systems, apparatus, instruments, which are real objects possessing material bases in existence; at the same time they are *processes* pursuing—within society and often against them—ends which no longer belong to anybody but which, as the alienating objectification of ends really pursued, become the objective, totalizing unity of *collective objects*.[60]

[60] *Ibid.*, pp. 162–163.

4. The Political Dimension: Individual and Polity

> The standpoint of the old type of materialism is civil society; the standpoint of the new materialism is human society or social humanity.
>
> KARL MARX
> *Theses on Feuerbach*

The Problem of "Individualism"

In the foregoing chapters, an attempt was made to delineate two qualitatively different conceptions of individuality and its relationship to sociality, conceptions which may respectively be called dialectical and metaphysical. Although some implications of these conceptions for political thought have been touched upon and others may be self-evident, it is possible to develop in greater detail examples of how theories of individuality may be elaborated into corresponding political doctrines; in other words, how a dialectical notion of individuality may be translated into a political doctrine of, as it were, "dialectical individualism," to be distinguished from "metaphysical individualism," based on a nondialectical notion of individuality.

First, some general remarks must be made concerning the term "individualism." The term is profoundly problematic, particularly because of the many hidden assumptions about man and society implicit in the word as it has come to be commonly used in Western liberal society.

The term "individualism" was apparently coined by Alexis de Tocqueville; and although it has come to have a meaning somewhat different—or, in any case, less precise—than he intended, his definition provides a provocative focal point for the present discussion:

Individualism is a novel expression, to which a novel idea has given birth. Our fathers were only acquainted with *égoisme* (selfishness). Selfishness is a passionate and exaggerated love of self, which leads a man to connect everything with himself and to prefer himself to everything in the world. Individualism is a mature and calm feeling, which disposes each member of the community to sever himself from the mass of his fellows and to draw apart with his family and his friends, so that after he has thus formed a little circle of his own, he willingly leaves society at large to itself. Selfishness originates in blind instinct, individualism proceeds from erroneous judgment more than from depraved feelings; it originates as much in deficiencies of mind as in perversity of heart.

Selfishness blights the germ of all virtue; individualism, at first, only saps the virtues of public life; but in the long run it attacks and destroys all others and is at length absorbed in downright selfishness. Selfishness is a vice as old as the world, which does not belong to one form of society more than another; individualism is of democratic origin. . . .[1]

Later in the book, de Tocqueville elaborates on his conception of men in an individualistic society:

Each of them, living apart, is a stranger to the fate of all the rest; his children and his private friends constitute to him the whole of mankind. As for the rest of his fellow citizens, he is close to them, but he does not feel them; he exists only in himself and for himself alone; and if his kindred still remain to him, he may be said at any rate to have lost his country.[2]

An "individualistic" society, then—to use currently popular terminology—is characterized by *privatization* and atomistic social relations, qualities which, if not synonymous with egoism in a narrower sense, always threaten to degenerate into it. We shall mention later the specifically political consequences—in terms, for example, of conceptions of the state and participation —that de Tocqueville attributes to such a society.

In contemporary popular usage, the term "individualism" has

1 Alexis de Tocqueville, *Democracy in America*, ed. Phillips Bradley (New York: Vintage Books, 1956), II, 104.
2 *Ibid.*, p. 336.

lost the special meaning, and with it the note of censure, attached to it by de Tocqueville. Instead, at least in the liberal democratic societies which are said to be characterized by individualism, the term—now one of moral approbation—seems to refer rather vaguely to a philosophy or a social system in which the individual has moral priority over the community and the central concern is individual freedom. Interestingly enough, however—and this is the crucial point—even in its new moral and more general sense, and for all its vagueness, the term tends to be applied even by dictionaries specifically to the type of social system represented by liberal democratic capitalist societies and to the antithetical relationship between individual and society that such a system implies. In short, the suggestion is that only a society so conceived can be regarded as embodying individual liberty. The typical opposition of individualism to socialism or collectivism reflects this tendency.

What has happened, in a sense, is that the popular conception of individualism has transformed de Tocqueville's atomistic society into a moral norm and his concept of privatization into the model of individual liberty. As this essay has been suggesting, it can be argued that this transformation is inherent in the liberal tradition from its inception. Nevertheless, if there is to be any meaning in the general concept of individualism as simply referring to any system of ideas that stresses the moral priority of the individual and his freedom, it should be possible to speak of other equally legitimate modes of individualism, based on conceptions of individuality and the relation between the individual and society different from those assumed by liberal-democratic doctrine, implying different conceptions of liberty, community, and the relationship between them.

The tendency to extend the liberal antithesis between individual and society to antitheses between derivatives of the words "individual" and "social" suggests a significant ramification of the liberal doctrine of individualism and its opposition to other possible forms of "individualism." There is a specific meaning to the fact that "individualism" and "socialism" are opposed to each other and that for liberal individualism it is a logical absurdity, a contradiction in terms, to speak of a socialist individualism—an individualism based on the view that the individual self-realization and development of all men can be achieved only through socialism, while capitalist individualism militates against fully realized individuality for all. The opposition of individualism to socialism simply reflects the central importance of the question of property to—indeed, its inseparability from—the problem of individualism. It has even been suggested, by John Dewey, for example, that the principles of property and its acquisition are all that now remain of the old liberal individualism:

> It is not too much to say that the whole significance of the older individualism has now shrunk to a pecuniary scale and measure. The virtues that are supposed to attend rugged individualism may be vocally proclaimed, but it takes no great insight to see that what is cherished is measured by its connection with those activities that make for success in business conducted for personal gain. Hence the irony of the gospel of "individualism" in business conjoined with suppression of individuality in thought and speech. One cannot imagine a bitterer comment on any professed individualism than that it subordinates the only creative individuality—that of the mind —to the maintenance of a regime which gives the few an opportunity for being shrewd in the management of monetary business.[3]

Dewey's claim may be somewhat exaggerated, but the fact remains that a particular doctrine of private property plays an essential role in all liberal versions of individualism, and that one of the primary forms that the antithesis between individual and society takes in liberal doctrine is a theory of property.

In any event, the concept of property serves very well to highlight the differences between our two modes of individualism, particularly since theories of property tend to embody concep-

[3] John Dewey, *Individualism Old and New* (New York: Capricorn Books, 1962), pp. 90–91.

tions of both liberty and community, together with their underlying concepts of man and the self. For example, the liberal conception of property, the earliest and foremost exponent of which is Locke,[4] can be said to reflect the principle of privatization, both as a principle of liberty and as a mode of community; so that the natural form of ownership is private, just as man is naturally private, and a man is free insofar as that "privatism" is respected. The other mode of individualism, of course, regards *communal* ownership, at least of the means of production, as the condition for *individual* liberation. Moreover, as we have already suggested, the liberal concept of property tends to reflect the objectification of man and the definition of freedom as compatible with subjection to objective forces external to man; while according to the other view, property can and must be organized in such a way as to overcome this kind of objectification.

An examination of the question of property in the light of our previous arguments concerning conceptions of selfhood and individuality may shed some light on these different theories. Discussions of property are often accompanied by the argument that man is by nature an appropriating and possessive animal. In more sophisticated form, such arguments sometimes even suggest that men achieve self-identity through appropriation, that the "I" is defined through the "my." Suggestions of this kind are sometimes used to justify private property—again, presumably, according to the principle that to act on what is "natural" is at least realistic, perhaps even morally good, and possibly divinely commissioned. The question to be raised here is whether or not —*even* if the naturalistic principle of morality is accepted and one proceeds from the premise that what is "natural" is "good" —the argument for private property can be derived from the con-

---

[4] In fact, it is possible to say that Locke is the only thinker to have worked out an elaborate philosophical justification of a "liberal" concept of property. His successors simply take for granted many of his conclusions, if not all their philosophical underpinnings, such as his concepts of natural rights and the state of nature, or the contract theory.

ception of man as appropriator without still other assumptions about human nature. It will be suggested here that one missing link in the argument is a particular conception of selfhood and individuality, a conception that is not self-evident, but without which the concept of appropriating man could just as easily be used, for example, to rationalize communal ownership.

This suggestion may be clarified by referring first to an argument proposed by John Dewey as he questions the legitimacy of deriving a particular doctrine of private property from the idea of an original proprietary instinct in man. Again, it is important to note that Dewey does not base his argument on a critique of the naturalistic morality that must be accepted as an original premise to make such a derivation reasonable. Nor does he question the existence or the importance of the proprietary instinct. Instead, he attacks the parochial, restricted conception of appropriation and the proprietary instinct that must be assumed to make the capitalist mode of private ownership a consequence of possessive human nature:

> No unprejudiced observer will lightly deny the existence of an original tendency to assimilate objects and events to the self, to make them part of the "me." We may even admit that the "me" cannot exist without the "mine." The self gets solidity and form through an appropriation of things which identifies them with whatever we call myself. Even a workman in a modern factory where depersonalization is extreme gets to have "his" machine and is perturbed at a change. Possession shapes and consolidates the "I" of philosophers. "I own, therefore I am" expresses a truer psychology than the Cartesian "I think, therefore I am." A man's deeds are imputed to him as their owner, not merely as their creator. That he cannot disown them when the moment of their occurrence passes is the root of responsibility, moral as well as legal.
>
>   But these same considerations evince the versatility of possessive activity. My wordly goods, my good name, my friends, my honor and shame all depend upon a possessive tendency. The need for appropriation has had to be satisfied: but only a calloused imagination fancies that the institution of private property as it exists A.D 1921 is the sole or indispensable means of its realization. Every gallant life is an experiment in different ways of fulfilling it. It expends

itself in predatory aggression, in forming friendships, in seeking fame, in literary creation, in scientific production. . . . We can conceive a state of things in which the proprietary impulse would get full satisfaction by holding goods as mine in just the degree in which they were visibly administered for a benefit in which a corporate community shared.

Does the case stand otherwise with the other psychological principle appealed to [in order to support the present system of property], namely, the need of an incentive of personal profit to keep men engaged in useful work? We need not content ourselves with pointing out the elasticity of the idea of gain, and possible equivalences for pecuniary gain, and the possibility of a state of affairs in which only those things would be counted personal gains which profit a group.[5]

Dewey's argument concerning the "versatility of possessive activity" can be pursued and elaborated from the particular perspective of this essay. As Dewey suggests, the equation that unites appropriating man with a doctrine of private property is doubtful in several ways. To begin with, it would seem that a particular conception of individuality and the self is implicit in the equation. Even if, as Dewey argues, appropriation to the self is essential to man—indeed, even if that appropriation must take the material form of property acquisition—more than one doctrine of property is compatible with that principle. There may be agreement concerning the importance for individuality of appropriation to the self, but the meaning of self-appropriation may vary according to the other ingredients which go into different theories of the self and the nature of individuation. For example, Dewey's notion that the individual proprietary impulse can be satisfied through group appropriation is particularly compatible with a dialectical view of individuality in which self-identity is inseparable from social consciousness and individuation is a truly social phenomenon. An insistence on private property as the only mode of appropriation suitable to human individuality would have to presuppose a "nondialec-

tical," exclusive conception of individuality, one in which, perhaps in a rather circular fashion, individuality is equated with
antisociality. Insofar as arguments for a particular system of
private property rely on a concept of human nature and a commitment to "individualism" or the moral primacy of the individual, it is not sufficient simply to point to a natural, universal, and immutable proprietary instinct in man. A particular
conception of the self and of individuality must be present to
support the claim that this instinct for appropriation to the
self can be expressed only in a particular way.

The "versatility" of the proprietary impulse, however, has
another dimension for Dewey. If the first argument can be said
to have focused on individuality and *community,* this one bears
particularly on individuality and *freedom.* As the quotation
cited above indicates, he argues not only that individual self-
appropriation can perhaps be achieved communally, but also
that appropriation can take a variety of forms other than acquisition of material property. Here again, our previous discussions of individuality may serve to shed light on Dewey's argument. It will be remembered that a distinction has been made
in this essay between ideas of individuality as "subjectivity," that
is, individuality defined in terms of self-activity and creativity
as internal impulses; and on the other hand, ideas which "objectify" individuality by making it a function of externalized
principles like *interest.* It can be argued that these same differences are reflected in different conceptions of self-appropriation.
One might say, for example, that property acquisition is objectified self-appropriation, that is, appropriation that can be
expressed only in external *objects,* material things; while
Dewey's notion that creative activity as such is a form of self-
appropriation seems to imply a conception of appropriation that
expresses subjectivity.

This point can perhaps be clarified by considering Marx's
ideas on labor and property. Marx does commend the political
economists beginning with Adam Smith for revealing the *"sub-*

jective essence of private property—*private property* as activity of itself, as *subject,* as person—" in the form of labor.[6] By making property a function of labor, they seem no longer to look upon property as a condition external to man. However, the outlook of political economy ultimately issues in a self-contradiction because it ends by objectifying "subjective" labor and thus objectifying man. Political economy begins by making property a function of human labor; but in its very essence—in its central ideas on the division of labor, class, the market mechanism, etc.— political economy necessarily ends by giving the *products* of labor, in the form of property and property relations, and even the *activity* of labor itself (labor sold as a commodity), an independent objective existence of which man then becomes a passive function. This is alienation, an inversion of the subject-object relationship,[7] in which objects attain mastery over subjects:

> . . . the object which labor produces—labor's product—confronts it as *something alien,* as a *power independent* of the producer. The product of labor is labor which has been embodied in an object, which has become material: it is the *objectification* of labor. Labor's realization is its objectification. In the sphere of political economy this realization of labor appears as *loss of realization* for the workers; objectification as *loss of the object* and *bondage to* it; appropriation as *estrangement,* as *alienation.* . . . The *alienation* of the worker in his product means not only that his labor becomes an object, an *external* existence, but that it exists *outside him,* independently, as something alien to him, and that it becomes a power on its own confronting him. It means that the life which he has conferred on the object confronts him as something alien and hostile.[8]

6 Karl Marx, *Economic and Philosophic Manuscripts of 1844,* trans. M. Milligan and ed. Dirk Struik (New York: International Publishers, 1964), p. 128.

7 See Shlomo Avineri, *The Social and Political Thought of Karl Marx* (Cambridge: Cambridge University Press, 1968), p. 103.

8 Marx, *op. cit.,* p. 108. In this passage, Marx makes it clear that he is using the term "objectification" in a neutral sense, and that objectification becomes "alienation" only under certain conditions. In the present essay, the term is being used—for lack of a better word and because the term is so

It is clear that this outlook—both the establishment of the "subjective essence" of property as a function of labor and the subsequent contradiction in the objectification of labor—appears before Adam Smith and the political economists in Locke's doctrine of property, as has been suggested in a previous chapter. It has already been noted how in Locke's political thought, and more elaborately in Smith's economic theories, property and the relations associated with it, relations culminating in the market system, take on an objective existence alien to man and ultimately determining his being. It can now be argued that, despite the emphasis placed on labor in these theories, their objectification of man and his activity makes it impossible for them to conceive of labor in anything but its externalized, objectified form—property. In this sense, property means not self-appropriation but self-alienation. The "subjective" view of appropriation, exemplified by Marx himself, continues to stress and develop the subjective aspect of labor, that is, human activity in all its expressions and generated by the self, not simply in its objectification in property and property relations operating, for example through the market mechanism, on impulses external to, independent of, and dominating over the individual.

This broad conception of appropriation suggested by Dewey and Marx still raises the question of what system of property, in the narrow, literal sense, is most suitable to the fulfillment of man's wider "proprietary" impulse. A Marxist, for example, might defend a socialist society precisely on the grounds that it best satisfies man's proprietary instinct—the proprietary instinct as self-activity and creativity—because only a socialist society can free man for creative self-development and widen the range of possibilities for productive self-affirmation. He would argue that the capitalist system of property, on the other hand, concerns

---

commonly used this way, even in discussions of Marx—to apply to the specific case in which "objectification [appears] as *loss of the object* and *bondage to it.*"

itself only with appropriation in a limited sense which, in fact, necessarily produces conditions inimical to individuality and self-realization by making man's activity alien and meaningless to him, by making his very selfhood a commodity, by confining his individuality to the externalized and restricted expression of his status in society or his function in the market system. Only a system that denies the primacy of appropriation in the narrow sense allows appropriation in the wider sense—the possession of a fully developed individuality. Thus, in this case, individualism means socialism.

A word of clarification should perhaps be interjected here. So far, there has been no consideration of the complications introduced into the contrast between these two conceptions of property by the fact that liberalism, particularly in its very earliest (Lockean) and very latest (welfare state) manifestations, permits a considerable degree of community control or state regulation of property, even to the extent of guaranteeing at least subsistence to everyone by taking from some in order to give to others. But to ignore the limits on the extent or, more precisely, the *intent* of control inherent in the liberal concept of property is to miss the point. Perhaps if we consider Locke's treatment of regulation of property, recalling that he is possibly the only thinker to provide an elaborate justification of the liberal conception of property and that his successors seem to have retained his conclusions while discarding much of the justification, it will become clear that the liberal concept of property is left fundamentally intact, even in the face of considerable government control, since the underlying principles of "privatism," "atomism," and "objectification" are still operative. In a previous chapter, there was an explanation of the sense in which Locke's concept of property reflected his "individualism." Now it will be seen that this "individualism" is virtually untouched by his doctrine of property regulation, a doctrine that some have argued permits an almost unlimited degree of regulation by the state, short of depriving men of their subsistence.[9]

There are two primary considerations to keep in mind in examining Locke's doctrine of property regulation: first, his argument, discussed earlier, concerning the legitimacy and consequences of class inequalities, and their priority over civil society; and, second, the underlying assumption of the contract whereby men enter civil society, discussed in the *Second Treatise*, that no rational being can rightfully be understood to have entered an agreement that would change his condition for the worse.

To begin with, if property and class differentials precede civil society and no rational man can be regarded as having intended to sacrifice his position by entering into civil society, one could say that a man's obligation to civil society extends only to the point where civil society violates those class differentials and his own position with respect to them. In other words, it is these differentials and their consequences, and not simply every man's inalienable right to subsistence, that constitute the ultimate limitation on government's right to interfere with property. The community not only must recognize every man's right to subsistence but also must respect the status differentials with which men enter civil society. Even if that right to subsistence is interpreted to mean that the community *owes* subsistence to all men, that debt must be limited by respect for those differentials. If it is said that this limitation is too vague to be meaningful, one could say the same about the subsistence standard. What, after all, constitutes an appropriate standard for subsistence? How much "meat, warmth, clothing, and shelter" are enough? One

---

9 Peter Laslett, for example, writes, "Even the minutest control of property by political authority can be reconciled with the doctrine of *Two Treatises*," in his introduction to Locke's *Two Treatises of Government* (New York: Mentor Books, 1965), p. 118. The discussion that follows here attempts, among other things, to show that arguments like that of Laslett simply miss some very fundamental points in Locke's doctrine.

must simply fall back, as Locke no doubt ultimately does, on some vague standard of "reasonableness" in judging when a man's rights have been violated. (In the case of the subsistence standard, surely one cannot wait until a man dies to determine whether or not he had been denied his right to subsistence; but short of that, there can be no definitive standard.)

A question then arises, of course, concerning the reconciliation of everyone's right to subsistence with everyone's right to preserve his position. If government has the right, even perhaps the duty, to regulate property to insure subsistence to everyone, what happens when this can be accomplished only by significantly worsening the condition of other members of the society? It seems clear that Locke's civil society is predicated on the condition that society has reached a level at which such a possibility no longer exists. The later stage of the state of nature, out of which civil society emerges, is precisely one in which gross property differentials have become compatible with subsistence for all. This is, after all, the significance of money. On the basis of Locke's premises, one would conclude that if society reverts to a condition in which some men must submit to a significant worsening of their condition to provide for the subsistence of other men, civil society has not served its purpose and men are again in the state of nature. Since the reason for entering the contract has been viodated, the contract is broken and obligation to the commonwealth dissolved.

In any case, to continue with the question of property regulation, leaving aside the problem of class as such: surely, if men enter civil society solely in order to *preserve* and *secure* the property they already have, it would be self-contradictory to suggest that government has a virtually unlimited right to interfere with property. Moreover, if Locke had intended to restrict the genuine right of property to the right of subsistence, it would hardly have been necessary to speak, as he does in the *Second Treatise*, of "estate" or "possessions" as a category distinct from "life" in the broad natural right of property, which includes

life, liberty, and possessions. One would speak only of the right
to life, and the right to the conditions necessary for its preservation would naturally follow. But Locke explicitly speaks of life,
liberty, and estate as distinct elements of the right of property
with which men enter civil society and the preservation of which
is the sole purpose of that society. In emphasizing Locke's wider
concept of property, one ought not forget that property in the
narrow sense is still a part of it. If, again, no rational man can
be expected to enter an agreement that would change his condition for the worse, this must apply to life, liberty, *and* possessions. Life is clearly the minimal condition—that is, everyone
has his person and his life—so government owes to everyone the
recognition of *that* right. But that is not to say that this is the
only right that government absolutely must respect. Some
people also have possessions as part of their "property." Men all
have an equal right to their property, but they do not all have
equal property. They may all have "equal" life and liberty, but
not possessions. For those without possessions, the natural right
to property does, in effect, mean only the right to subsistence;
for those with possessions, it means more. This also affects
Locke's theory concerning the right of rebellion. Since men
enter civil society with unequal possessions for civil society to
preserve, the contract in effect promises different things to different people. Hence, a condition of life that would justify
rebellion for some would not for others.

One might also ask why Locke would take such pains to attack the notion that property is a conventional, rather than a
natural, right, if his right of property is to be so severely restricted. After all, anyone arguing that the right to property is
simply a convention would most likely draw the line at society's
right to deprive men of their lives; nor is the argument that the
community positively owes subsistence to every man less compatible with this view, provided that the natural right to life is
recognized. Indeed, it may be more compatible. (Even Hobbes
grants man a natural right of self-preservation, although prop-

erty for him is simply a conventional right.)

As for what can be done by rule of the majority, which represents the "consent" necessary to allow interference with any
man's property, it simply cannot be argued consistently that the
scope of majority rule is virtually unlimited. The point is precisely that, if nothing else, the conditions of the contract determine the boundaries within which government can operate,
and limits are placed on the interpretation of "consent" by the
principle that "no rational Creature can be supposed to change
his condition with an intention to be worse." [10] No man can be
interpreted to have consented to majority rule to the point
where majority rule would mean a significant worsening of his
condition.

To summarize, Locke's conception of property rights can
perhaps be formulated this way: (1) Natural right established
the equal right to the preservation of one's property (the equal
right: not the right to equal property, but the equal right to the
protection of what one has). (2) Consent to money—or the situation it represents—established a right to unequal property, etc.
Both are prior to civil society and *both* establish limiting conditions on civil society.

Nor can one simply dismiss the significance of money by
pointing out that consent established only a positive, not a
natural, right. To begin with, the agreement to money exists
prior to civil society and must be a limiting condition on it,
just as any prior contract is a limitation on any subsequent contract. The important consideration is that, since Locke makes a
particular point of associating consent to money with consent to
its consequences, we are forced to conclude that, as long as
money is accepted, its consequences are accepted. The agreement remains binding and could only be considered abrogated
if money were abolished. In short, the right of property, as
such, is natural; the specific content of that right may not be
"naturally" determined, but the content given to it by the "pre-

10 Locke, *ibid.*, p. 398 (art. 131).

civil" agreement still has moral priority over civil society. In effect, then, Locke's "individualistic" model of society, as it was described in chapter 3, establishes the limits on government's right to control private property.

"Civil Society" and "Human Society"

In any case, different conceptions of individualism must, needless to say, be expressed in different principles of social and political organization. If we are to draw a distinction between "metaphysical" and "dialectical" individualism, then, we should be able to delineate a mode of society appropriate to each. Perhaps Marx's distinction between "civil society" and "human society" can be seen in this light. This distinction will at the same time draw our attention more directly to the possible connections between certain theories of mind and certain social doctrines and thus bring us full circle.

Reference has already been made to Marx's ideas about the activity of mind and the relation between subject and object. It will be remembered that his theory of consciousness involved a reunification of subject and object through subjective activity, the active participation of the subject in the objective world. His critique of earlier materialism—what we might call "metaphysical" materialism—and the metaphysical empiricism on which it is based centers largely on the gap between subject and object and on the passive, responsive role of the subject which these theories assume. He praises idealism for its albeit imperfect attempt to reunite subject and object by its emphasis on the interpenetration of subject and object based on the active role of the subject. Marx then goes on to translate this epistemological idea of the active subject into his views on individual self-activity, creative self-realization, and the autonomy of man in society.

The *Theses on Feuerbach,* in which these ideas are rather elliptically outlined, explicitly establishes a direct connection between epistemological considerations and Marx's theory of politics and society. Having sketched his critique of early empiricist materialism and his praise of the idealist emphasis on subjectivity and activity,[11] Marx continues: "The standpoint of the old type of materialism is civil society; the standpoint of the new materialism is human society or social humanity." [12]

These rather epigrammatic statements and the connections they seek to outline between epistemology and social theory can be understood in several ways. First, a brief summary of some possible interpretations, which will be explained in greater detail later on. To begin with, we have already alluded to a possible connection between Lockean empiricism, which is the basis of the "old" materialism, and a conception of society as a network of objective forces—class, role, later the market mechanism, etc.—of which man is largely a receptive function. Marx is highly critical of this view, perhaps less with respect to its accuracy as a mode of analysis, at least in a given historical period, than with respect to the dehumanized reality it reflects and the tendency to universalize, legitimize, and perpetuate that reality, to regard it as a necessary condition. Marx seeks to substitute for this view of society a conception that reflects a possible new reality, a conception that emphasizes the possibility of man's "subjective," self-active mastery and transcendence of these objective forces. In short, Marx is critical of the old empiricist-materialist conception because it is in its very essence a denial of the possibility of such mastery and transcendence. "Civil society" from this perspective, then, reflects the society of "objectified" man; while "human society" is the society in which man has achieved mastery over history, that is, in which man has left the stage of "prehistory" and entered "human history."

From a slightly different, though related, perspective, Marx's emphasis on "subjectivity" and the epistemological theory of

---

11 See above, pp. 33–34.
12 Marx, *Theses on Feuerbach*, in Karl Marx, *Selected Writings in Sociology and Social Philosophy*, ed. T. B. Bottomore and M. Rubel (Harmondsworth: Penguin Books, 1963), Thesis X, p. 84.

the active subject are reflected in his conception of man as an active creative being with an internal need for complete self-realization. Here the reunification of subject and object takes the form of individual creativity and man's active relationship to the environment through all his faculties. This concept of man becomes the basis of Marx's moral commitment to man's *right* to creative self-development; and this commitment establishes another connection between the theory of mind and the social and political doctrines, in the sense that Marx outlines the social conditions necessary for the implementation of the right to self-development, the social conditions which alone make possible for all men the reunification of subject and object in the form of creative activity. Again, these conditions are expressed in the formula "human society."

Finally, from an explicitly political point of view, Marx makes it clear that his ideas specifically on politics and the state can also be understood as expressing the need for reunification of subject and object and the emphasis on the active subject. In this sense, "the dualism between individual life and species life, between the life of civil society and political life," [13] reflects the dualism between subject and object, political power representing an alienation of social power from individual men and the abstraction and objectification of that power in the form of the state to which individuals are coercively subjected. The principle of society expressed in the concept of "civil society," then, reflects a dualism between individual men and social power, the alienation of social power in the form of political power and the state. Marx's principle of "human society" involves the reappropriation by the individual of social power, and thus the abolition of *political* power, which is simply alienated, objectified social power over and against the individual.

The present discussion will concentrate on this latter perspec-

---

[13] Marx, "On the Jewish Question," in *Writings of the Young Marx on Philosophy and Sociology,* trans. and ed. L. D. Easton and K. H. Guddat (Garden City, N.Y.: Anchor Books, Doubleday and Co., 1967), p. 23.

tive. The first aspect of Marx's argument—that dealing with society as a network of objective forces—has been touched upon earlier and will be dealt with here only in connection with other aspects of the argument. Before the more specifically political argument is considered, however, a few words should be devoted to Marx's conception of creative man. This aspect of Marx's thought, centering on his concept of alienation, is by now familiar, especially to readers of commentaries on Marx which have appeared in the last decade; but a brief summary may still be useful.

Alienation, which is at the heart of Marx's social doctrine, can be said to mean in general the separation of subject and object through man's passive experience of the world and himself.[14] This separation and passivity take several forms, only one of which is the loss of social autonomy and agency with respect to the state. More immediately, alienation takes the form of man's estrangement from his own activity, his loss of creativity through meaningless, fragmented labor, and, in general, man's failure actively to experience the world through all human faculties. It is clear that here Marx expands the notion of the active subject into a general concept of active, creative man; and, of course, this concept of man has social and political implications. On this concept of creative man Marx bases his notion of human freedom as involving the right to creative self-fulfillment, a right that can be exercised only in a particular kind of society. The proper social conditions must be present in order to allow men to overcome alienation, not only in the political sense, but in a more direct and personal sense, by becoming active, self-creative, productive beings whose individuality is fully and broadly developed.

The emancipated man is one who experiences his environment positively and totally through all his faculties and does not live simply the fragmented, partial existence of a creature

14 See Erich Fromm, *Marx's Concept of Man* (New York: Frederick Ungar Publishing Co., 1961), p. 44.

whose activity is dictated almost entirely by the division of labor. Moreover, he is a man whose activities have a subjective, *human* meaning arising out of an internal need to act creatively, to act for the sake of the activity itself, not simply for the sake of some external force alien to the activity itself—things, commodities, capital, property—nor because of coercion by other men, by physical needs, or even by the imperatives of sheer survival. And, again, the free man is one whose identity is a subjectively meaningful *human* identity, not simply an alien identity assigned to him by the objective forces of the market, the class system, the division of labor, etc. Thus, human emancipation requires a form of society that allows freedom from subjection to things, property, alien social forces, and permits transcendence of the division of labor. Marx is seeking a form of association in which men, through their combined and cooperative labor, can not only achieve mastery over objective social and economic conditions, but also free themselves to a great extent from social labor so that they can pursue a variety of creative activities. In a society where labor is no longer directed solely toward production for the sake of profit, it is possible to conceive of men whose lives are not completely devoted to fragmented social labor. The cooperative efforts of the community should permit men who indeed can, according to Marx's famous formula, be "farmers in the morning, fishermen in the afternoon, critics in the evening"—in short, men who are creatively active in a total sense. Here, again, to quote Herbert Marcuse, the new "human" society for Marx

> ... is the definitive resolution of the antagonism between man and nature, and between man and man. It is the true solution of the conflict between existence and essence, between objectification and self-affirmation, between freedom and necessity, between individual and species.[15]

In short, the new society is the resolution of the opposition between subject and object.

[15] Herbert Marcuse, quoted in *ibid.*, p. 27.

It is worth noting in passing that Marx is not alone in associating an epistemology that emphasizes the activity of the subject with certain moral and social ideas based on man's essential
creativity. A particularly striking example of such an association
is again provided by Humboldt. It may also be worth pointing
out that Noam Chomsky, who in *Cartesian Linguistics* draws
attention to the connection between Humboldt's theory of language (which is in essence his theory of mind) and his political
ideas, himself seems prepared to draw similar moral and political conclusions from his own theory of language as an expression
of the active, creative quality of mind.[16]

Chomsky emphasizes that Humboldt's conception of language
must be examined in the context of his social and political
thought and the concept of human nature they reflect. The
point here is that Humboldt's conception of human liberty is
grounded in the idea that man has a right to fulfill his essential
creative nature, the nature that is best exemplified by the spontaneous and creative qualities of language. Humboldt's doctrine
of political liberty, writes Chomsky, "is based on his advocacy of
the fundamental human rights to develop a personal individuality through meaningful creative work and unconstrained
thought." [17] He goes on to quote Humboldt himself:

> Naturally, freedom is the necessary condition without which even
> the most soul-satisfying occupation cannot produce wholesome
> effects. . . . Whatever task is not chosen of man's free will, whatever
> constrains or even only guides him, does not become part of his own
> nature. It remains forever alien to him; if he performs it, he does
> so not with true humane energy but with mere mechanical skill. . . .
> . . . all peasants and craftsmen could be transformed into *artists*,
> i.e., people who love their craft for its own sake, who refine it with
> their self-guided energy and inventiveness, and in so doing cultivate
> their own intellectual energies, ennoble their character, and increase

16 It is significant, too, that Chomsky explicitly opposes his doctrine of the
active, creative mind to modern behavioral doctrines of the passive, receptive mind, just as the Kantian approach is opposed to the "older" empiricism.
17 Noam Chomsky, *Cartesian Linguistics: A Chapter in the History of Ra-
tionalist Thought* (New York: Harper and Row, 1966), p. 24.

their enjoyments. This way humanity would be ennobled by the very things which now, however beautiful they might be, degrade it.[18]

Freedom for Humboldt, then, consists in self-realization, subjectively meaningful creative activity arising spontaneously out of an inner need of man's creative nature. And it is on this conception of freedom that he bases his idea of political liberty. Like Marx, he begins with a concept of the activity of mind, expands the principle of the active creative subject into a concept of practical activity reflected in creative work, and then derives from this a concept of freedom and social liberty grounded in man's need for individuality and self-realization through meaningful creative activity.[19]

Returning, then, to Marx, we can now proceed to a consideration of his argument in its most immediately political form. Like Hegel in the *Philosophy of Right*, Marx distinguishes between civil society and the state and goes on to argue that the very nature of society as represented by civil society, while it necessitates the existence of the state, at the same time involves a split, a contradition between civil society and the state. Civil society represents the private realm, the "sphere of egoism," the struggle of individual private interests, the *bellum omnium contra omnes*, the social interaction of egoistic, alienated individuals whose relationships are essentially the externalized, atomistic, utilitarian relations of the market. Since at the level of society individuals are egoistic and solely "private" in the sense that their interests, insofar as they are mutually antagonistic, must ultimately conflict with the general interest; since society is an expression of men's separation from each other as much as their community with each other; since, in other words, man cannot universalize his individuality, the general interest must exist as an abstraction separate from and alien to individ-

18 Wilhelm von Humboldt, quoted in *ibid.*, p. 25.
19 Chomsky refers to some of these similarities between Humboldt and Marx, and even points out certain affinities with Rousseau. See *ibid.*, p. 91, n. 51.

uals and their daily life in society. That abstracted general interest must, then, be represented by the state, so that community exists for the most part only in the abstract, objectified, alien, and coercive form of the state. Man is split into public and private, and, moreover, his public "self" is separated from him in the objectified form of political power which is antagonistic to him. Here is how Marx expresses it:

> By its nature the perfected political state is man's *species-life* in *opposition* to his material life. All the presuppositions of this egoistic life remain in *civil society outside* the state, but as qualities of civil society. Where the political state has achieved its full development, man leads a double life, a heavenly and an earthly life, not only in thought or consciousness but in *actuality*. In the *political community* he regards himself as a communal being; but in civil society he is active as a *private individual*, treats other men as means, reduces himself to a means, and becomes the plaything of alien powers. The political state is as spiritual in relation to civil society as heaven is in relation to earth. It stands in the same opposition to civil society and goes beyond it in the same way as religion goes beyond the limitation of the profane world, that is, by recognizing, reestablishing, and necessarily allowing itself to be dominated by it. In his *innermost* actuality, in civil society, man is a profane being. Here, where he counts as an actual individual to himself and others, he is an *illusory* phenomenon. In the state where he counts as a species-being, on the other hand, he is an imaginary member of an imagined sovereignty, divested of his actual individual life and endowed with an unactual universality.[20]

Thus, in one sense, man is split into two contradictory and antagonistic elements: man as individual and man as citizen, particular and universal, subjective and objective. In an even more concrete sense, in actuality, man's "universal" communal being takes on an existence abstracted and independent of his individual life and becomes hypostatized in the state. It is, of course, true that man has been emancipated relative, for example, to his position in feudal society, since his individual life, the "principle of subjectivity," has achieved a degree of primacy in

[20] Marx, "On the Jewish Question," pp. 225–226.

the context of civil society, and the state is even seen as an instrument of individual interest, a function of civil society. Nevertheless, the very nature of civil society and of man's private life in civil society means that, insofar as the "unactual universality" of his individual life must be actualized in the form of a common interest, as it necessarily must be if man is to live in political society, it must be done by a power alien to him, at best through his participation in a fictional community which is antagonistic to his *real* life and must be enforced from without. In short, even the ideal, perfected political state, in the form of an ideal liberal democracy, means a violation of individual freedom and a denial of *human,* as opposed to simply political, emancipation. In practice, the situation is even worse, since the state as a function of interest and of civil society—which is necessarily a class society —inevitably becomes the state as an instrument of one class to be used against another, the tool of a ruling class. In such a case, the general interest, even in its abstract and alien form, is not actualized, and only individuals who are members of the ruling class are even *politically* emancipated.

At this point, it is important to recall the significance of Marx's historical perspective and his dynamic conceptions of man and society. For him, civil society is, of course, a historical phenomenon associated with particular material conditions, and man as he is in this context is not "natural man," but simply man specifically as a member of civil society. It will be remembered that the case is quite different, for example, with Locke, who may certainly be regarded as one of the original philosophers of civil society. It has already been suggested that Locke makes no fundamental distinction between "natural man" and man in civil society, that he has no fundamentally dynamic conception of man. In essence, "natural man" is simply abstracted from civil society. It is therefore difficult for Locke to conceive of a principle of society more suitable to human nature than civil society, and he must establish a principle of politics based on the particular kind of relationship between private and public, individual and community, that exists in civil society. Marx, however, seeks his "natural man" beneath what he feels to be the second nature imposed upon man by his existence in civil society. It is precisely because he is able to conceive of a different "human nature," a different form of individuality than the one abstracted from civil society, that Marx can go beyond civil society and develop his principle of "human society," a principle not bound by the particular limitations of civil society, its cleavages, antagonisms, and alienation.

The object of this new "human society," then, is human emancipation, the full and free development of individuality. To achieve this objective, the limitations of civil society must be transcended. According to Marx, these limitations consist in the fact that in civil society, to quote one commentary,

> . . . man's own activity in government, wealth, and culture becomes to him an alien power, standing over against him instead of being ruled by him. The remedy is communism, a "real community" in which the contradiction between the separate individual or family and the interest of all has been overcome by healing the cleavage between production and consumption, between intellectual and manual labor, arising from division of labor in modern industry. This requires the abolition of the state, social classes, and all existing forms of association that express man's self-alienation. The alien and seemingly independent powers that fetter men—the state, class, industry, religion—are to be brought under their control so there is nothing independent of self-active, associated individuals.[21]

Communist society's contribution to individuality and self-activity is really twofold. On the one hand, it restores individual autonomy by freeing man from subjection to alien powers—human, institutional, and material. On the other hand—although this is perhaps simply an elaboration of the previous point—it provides a form of association through which men can unite their powers in such a way as to transcend—rather than to intensify, rigidify, and objectify—the division of labor. It is only by minimizing the socially enforced division of labor that men

[21] Easton and Guddat, Introduction to *Writings of the Young Marx*, p. 24.

can express themselves fully through all their faculties, only thus that they can get beyond what Marx calls the transformation of personal into material powers; so that only through the *community*, properly constituted, can men achieve *individuality*. As has already been suggested, men can achieve freedom, autonomy, individuality, and self-realization only when they are no longer defined in terms of the objective conditions of their roles in the division of labor and the market—in short, when they become active as *persons*, in a sense as *subjects* rather than as *objects*. This can happen only in a particular social context which transcends the conditions of civil society, including its political expression, the objectification and alienation of society in the form of the state:

> Only when the actual, individual man has taken back into himself the abstract citizen and in his everyday life, his individual work, and his individual relationship has become a *species-being*, only when he has recognized and organized his own powers as *social* powers so that social force is no longer separated from him as *political* power, only then is human emancipation complete.[22]

It is crucial to note, then, that the consequence of this reunification of public and private (objective and subjective) is *not* the abstraction, objectification, and idealization of society over and against the individual which the popular conception of Marx often attributes to his doctrine. On the contrary, it is the reappropriation of society by the individual, a restoration of individual autonomy to men living in society. The "social" or "general" must have no existence independent of the individual or particular, and therefore cannot be represented by a power alien to individual men. The conditions of society must be such that this cleavage is no longer inevitable, so that instead of the "public" being authoritatively imposed upon the "private" from without, public and private will both originate in the individual. The object of Marx's social revolution is, in effect, to make

22 Marx, "On the Jewish Question," p. 241.

it possible, through the healing of fundamental social antagonisms, for the individual to become the source of universality instead of the plaything of a universality or objectivity externally imposed.

It is instructive to contrast Marx's views on this score with those of liberalism and to note that he is here touching upon an essential aspect of liberal theories of the state which is usually overlooked. In a sense, it may be argued that the positions generally ascribed to liberalism, on the one hand, and Marx (and often Rousseau), on the other, may be reversed. Criticism of Marxism, like attacks on Rousseau's concept of the general will, sometimes suggest that it has totalitarian implications because it allegedly gives society an existence independent of its members, and the common good a meaning above and beyond the good of the individuals constituting it. For liberalism, on the other hand, society is presumed to be simply the sum of its parts and the "public interest" essentially a sum of private interests, so that individuals take precedence over society. Actually, it is possible to argue that it is the liberals, and not Marx or Rousseau, who objectify society in the form of the state. Enough has already been said about the sense in which liberalism tends to confer upon society—for example in the form of class relations, the division of labor, and particularly the market mechanism— an objective existence independent of its individual members. Now it can be suggested that a similar principle applies to liberal political doctrines. It is precisely for liberalism, because of its particular view of the nature of man and society, that the public interest must be something abstracted and separate from private interests; it must, in fact, be represented and objectified by a power external and alien to the mass of private individuals, i.e. by the state, be it the authoritarian monarchy of Hobbes, who is in so many essential ways the father of liberalism, or the more obviously liberal representative governments of Locke, Madison, or Mill. It can, of course, simply be pointed out that an aggregate of private interests (and presumably for liberalism the public interest ideally is such an aggregate) must always and necessarily be something different from a mere *sum* of private interests, perhaps in much the same way that Hegel's history "cunningly" produces something quite different and separate from a subjectively meaningful "sum" of individual acts and takes on an independent objective existence and meaning. At best, an "aggregate" of interests is a rather unreal abstraction. At worst, the concept of a *sum* of private interests, particularly a sum of conflicting private interests, is a logical absurdity.[23] But aside from this, there is a great deal more in liberal theories of government and representation that simply does not bear out the claim that the public interest does not assume an objectified independent existence distinct from the interests of individual men.

In this connection, Hobbes provides a significant key to the nature of liberalism. He is, in a sense, the first philosopher of civil society, the first important thinker systematically to conceive of society as a network of interacting and conflicting egoistic interests and to regard politics as a function of interest. For Hobbes, it is precisely because the area of commonality among individual interests is so minimal and because men cannot universalize their private interests or achieve a sufficiently broad concert of wills, that the sovereign is called upon to represent a public interest conducive to, but at the same time transcending, all private interests. That interest is public precisely insofar as it does transcend all private interests. Men are above all private beings, and the crucial point here is that their public being must be expressed not by themselves, but by an external power, the sovereign armed with the coercive force of the state. In a sense, the sovereign is the public interest objectified and personified.

What may be less obvious is that even more liberal theories of

---

23 It would seem that a popular way of resolving this logical difficulty has been to identify the public interest with the private interests of a particular class—at least implicitly and often rather explicitly, as seems to be the case with Locke, and, as we shall see, with other liberals as well.

the state are based on assumptions very similar to those of Hobbes, on similar conceptions of civil society and the split between the private realm of civil society and the public realm of the state. For example, Locke, who seems to subscribe to some notion of a harmony of self-interest, nevertheless cannot rely on the invisible hand of this harmonious interplay, nor even on some form of popular government, but requires an elite body of "prudent" men to represent and embody the common good, men who are suitable for office precisely to the degree that they can transcend the narrowness of private interests.[24] Madison, too, depends upon "the substitution of representatives whose enlightened views and virtuous sentiments render them superior to local prejudices and to schemes of injustice."[25] Significantly, this observation concerning "enlightened" and "virtuous" representatives appears as an elaboration of Madison's famous, and seemingly contradictory, argument that one must ensure institutional protections against the fact that "Enlightened statesmen will not always be at the helm."[26] He proposes such an institutional protection in the form of a *large* republic which will, among other things, enlarge the choice of possible representatives and thereby encourage the selection of enlightened and virtuous men who are superior to special interests: ". . . if the proportion of fit characters be not less in the large than in the small republic, the former will present a greater option, and consequently a greater probability of a fit choice."[27] (It must be remembered, too, that Madison explicitly supports a large republic precisely on the grounds that it will *prevent* the kind of harmony of interest democracy requires—that is, in a sense, on the grounds that such a republic would, by increasing the diver-

[24] As was suggested in footnote 23, it is more than possible to equate these prudent, disinterested men with a particular class, the class of propertied "gentlemen."

[25] James Madison, Federalist No. 10, in *The Federalist* (New York: Modern Library, 1950), p. 61.

[26] *Ibid., p. 57.*

[27] *Ibid.,* p. 60.

sity and antagonisms of interest, *insure* that only the most "extraordinary" men could overcome those antagonisms sufficiently to represent the "public interest.") In other words, he proposes a form of institution in which the small proportion of representatives relative to the total population will more accurately reflect the actual proportion between the very few extraordinary men who can be expected to act in the public interest and the masses of "private" men who cannot. In short, a large union has the advantage of necessitating a representative, rather than a democratic, form of government, and also of increasing the likelihood of "enlightened" representatives. This means that it has the essential advantage of reducing the proportion of men who will be asked to represent the public interest. Whatever Madison's convictions may be regarding the likelihood of "enlightened statesmen," then, his argument certainly emphasizes the distance between private and public interest.[28]

28 In his proposal that the representative body consist solely of merchants, men of property, and members of the "learned professions," Madison's colleague Alexander Hamilton emphasizes this separation. On the one hand, he confirms the impression that only a group of enlightened men can truly represent the public interest, by suggesting that selected members of the "learned professions," who "form no distinct interest in society" (*Federalist* No. 35, *ibid.*, p. 214) are the appropriate impartial arbiters between conflicting private interests and will promote the "general interests" (see *ibid.*, p. 215). On the other hand, Hamilton suggests that the *private* interests of certain classes of men—tradesmen and others involved in manufacture and commerce—be promoted, not by themselves, but by their "natural representatives": "They know that the merchant is their natural patron and friend; and they are aware, that however great the confidence they may justly feel in their own good sense, their interests can be more effectually promoted by the merchant than by themselves. . . . We must therefore consider merchants as the natural representatives of all these classes of the community" (*ibid.*, p. 213). In this argument, Hamilton puts an even greater distance between the public interest and the masses of men, placing one more step between them and the implementation of the common interest: even their private interests must be represented by more "enlightened" individuals, whose more enlightened private interests must in turn be transformed into a public interest by truly disinterested and superior men. In a sense, then, his proposal synthesizes the two forms in which liberalism most commonly objectifies the public interest: the embodiment of the public interest by a group of extraordinary men *and* its identification with the private interests of a minority class.

To anticipate the objection that Locke and Madison demand disinterested representatives only because a true aggregate of private interests requires transcendence of any particular one, it can only be repeated that a "public interest" that transcends all "local prejudices" and private interests, or consolidates all conflicting interests into a self-consistent public expression (if this is even possible), will necessarily be something rather different from any private interest or any sum of all such interests. The significant point, however, is that Locke and Madison formulate their theories in such a way as to emphasize the separateness of the public realm from, even its inaccessibility to, the mass of private men. The separation between public and private is concretely objectified in the form of an actual separation between the mass of ordinary "private" individuals and a distinct class of more extraordinary men who in their persons embody the public interest, the transcendence of the private realm. It is important to note that the majority of men—either because of their original "private" natures or because of the competitive and exclusive egoism, the "privatization," imposed upon them by an objectified, independently existing socioeconomic system—*cannot,* in fact, express their own "public" selves. In a very important sense, the role of the representative body is not simply to reflect the private interests of its constituents, but, as it were, to embody their fictional public beings.

One might object that it is unjust to generalize about liberalism on the basis of two of its earlier and least democratic exponents. The point, however, is that the tendency to separate and objectify the public realm here attributed to Locke and Madison is inherent in the most fundamental assumptions of liberalism and applies to its more democratic theorists as well. J. S. Mill, often regarded as the supreme liberal, is a striking case in point.[29] For Mill, not only is the public interest not expressed

29 Even Bentham, perhaps the first "democratizer" of liberalism and the thinker who is often cited as the prime exponent of a public interest which is nothing more than the sum of its parts, suggests a similar élitism. To be-

by private individuals, even their representative assembly does not express the public will. Interestingly enough, the representatives are unqualified to make public policy, to embody the public will, precisely to the extent that they *are* qualified to represent the desires and private interests of the people; while the true governors and the legislative council are qualified to rule precisely to the extent that they are disqualified to act as representatives of the people—that is, to the extent that they are by virtue of their superiority *different* from the majority of men and thus unable truly to reflect their interests:

> But the very fact which most unfits such bodies [popular assemblies] for a Council of Legislation, qualifies them the more for their other office—namely, that they are not a selection of the greatest political minds in the country, from whose opinions little could with certainty be inferred concerning those of the nation, but are, when properly constituted, a fair sample of every grade of intellect among the people which is at all entitled to a voice in public affairs. Their part is to indicate wants, be an organ for popular demands. . . .[30]

The paradoxical union of democratic and undemocratic, authoritarian, or elitist ideas in Mill has always been a matter of concern to his interpreters. It should be apparent, however, that the paradox is not peculiar to Mill and that his undemo-

---

gin with, we must repeat the question as to whether the "sum" of private interests can ever be very much more than an illusive abstraction. More specifically, however, Bentham's utilitarianism suggests nothing if not a kind of mildly authoritarian rule by expertise, in which the public interest and the finer points of the principle of utility are accessible only to the experts (presumably, social scientists) to whose authority the masses of ordinary men defer. This certainly tends to emphasize the separateness and abstraction of the public interest from private interests. It is also worth noting that, despite the fact that it is man's right to have narrow private interests, the possession of such interests—which now become "sinister" interests—disqualifies one for public office. Since it is impossible, and indeed undesirable, for most men not to possess such private interests, the public interest is the property of a very select few. (See Bentham's *Handbook of Political Fallacies* for a rather entertaining discussion of those classes of men who are least capable of transcending sinister interests.)

30 John Stuart Mill, *On Representative Government*, introd. F. A. Hayek (Chicago: Henry Regnery Co., 1962), p. 113.

cratic inclinations are not simply idiosyncratic but are to a greater or lesser extent basic to all liberal democratic doctrines, insofar as they are founded on the kind of conceptions of public and private here outlined. The tendency exemplified by the three above-mentioned thinkers is not accidental, but can be regarded as inherent in the fundamental assumptions of liberalism. To begin with, as has already been suggested, society as conceived by the liberals is so constructed that the majority of men, either by nature or conditioned as they are by participation in the competitive society, the class system, the market, etc., *cannot* become the "prudent," "virtuous," or superior men who can transcend private interests or whose private interests do not necessarily conflict with the general interest, men who can in their own persons represent both their private and public selves. In part, liberalism, can circumvent the problems inherent in this view by taking the position that an absolutely essential aspect of freedom is freedom from politics: not simply freedom from government but freedom from *politics*, that is, the right to remain private, to maintain one's egoism and remain engrossed in domestic concerns.[31] According to this conception of freedom, even political participation, which would seem to be the ultimate expression of *public* life, for the citizen of a liberal democratic state takes on a uniquely *private* meaning. Political participation consists of registering private interests, while the state represents the public will. The free man, as man, as member of civil society, even as *citizen,* is private; only the state is "public." It is not simply that liberalism permits apathy or regards it as "functional" in a democratic society, as do certain modern liberal social scientists like Seymour Martin Lipset. The point is that for liberalism even the active citizen is conceived as essentially private and a political act like voting becomes "privatized." Indeed, it can be argued that the more liberalism has

---

[31] This is perhaps what some modern social critics might call "privatization." But while they diagnose it as a symptom of social pathology, for the liberals the right to "privatization" is the better part of liberty.

broadened the base of electoral representation and the more it has diffused access to the political realm, the more private has participation necessarily become. The vote, which is the highest political act available to most citizens, has increasingly become not an act of participation in the political realm, but an act of withdrawal from it, an abdication of political responsibility to the representative so that the citizen can return to the pursuit of private interests (or perhaps it would be more accurate to call it a ratification by the citizen of his inevitable loss of responsibility). This mode of "passive" democracy would seem to be justified in terms of the liberal doctrine of liberty.

The attraction, indeed the genius, of liberalism perhaps lies in this conception of political liberty. Liberalism has found, in its unique idea of "private" political participation, a way of dealing with man's apparent desire to see his interests served through society while at the same time preserving the exclusiveness of his ego and his private interests, a way of synthesizing man's need for at least an appearance of autonomy with his apparent need for authority, his desire to "escape from freedom." This is perhaps the advantage that liberal democracy has over doctrines of participatory democracy. The irony of liberalism is that privatization, the possibility of which is considered so essential to liberty, becomes not simply a *possibility*, but a virtual necessity for the majority of men; and that, because liberal doctrine assumes an antagonism between private and public, individual and community, the individual freedom it calls for can paradoxically be achieved only at the price of subjection to an external, alien public power, a power ultimately inimical to individual liberty and autonomy. Again, there seems to be an inherent contradiction that cannot, in the end, be resolved.[32]

---

[32] It is undeniable that liberalism, in its conception of freedom as privatization, takes account of what seems to be an important aspect of human nature, which the advocates of participatory democracy would do well to consider. The problem, however, is not as simple as, for example, a modern liberal like Isaiah Berlin makes it when he pleads for the right of privatization (especially in his introduction to the *Four Essays on Liberty*). The difficulty

Again, de Tocqueville provides a fascinating commentary on the nature and consequences of a society based on principles like those attributed here to the British liberals. Here he discusses the dangers to liberty posed by "privatization":

> It is not necessary to do violence to such a people in order to strip them of the rights they enjoy; they themselves willingly loosen their hold. The discharge of political duties appears to them to be a troublesome impediment which diverts them from their occupations and business. If they are required to elect representatives, to support the government by personal service, to meet on public business, they think they have no time, they cannot waste their precious hours in useless engagements; such idle amusements are unsuited to serious men who are engaged with the more important interests of life. These people think they are following the principle of self-interest, but the idea they entertain of that principle is a very crude one; and the better to look after their own business, they neglect their chief business, which is to remain their own masters.[33]

Later, de Tocqueville shows how "individualism "or "privatization" can lead to the objectification, and ultimately despotism, of the state:

> Hence such men can never, without an effort, tear themselves from their private affairs to engage in public business; their natural bias leads them to abandon the latter to the sole visible and permanent representative of the interests of the community; that is to say, to the state.[34]

These remarks are, of course, very close to Rousseau's critique of privatization in the liberal state and the loss of autonomy it

---

lies in the fact that liberalism may convert the *right* into a necessity. In any case, the liberal conception of society certainly underestimates another perhaps equally important aspect of human nature—the inclination toward what Hannah Arendt calls "public happiness," the unique happiness of acting in the political space (see, for example, her *On Revolution* [New York: The Viking Press], 1965, chap. 3). Perhaps, in the final analysis, the doctrine of liberal democracy is more attractive than that of participatory democracy, but it may also be the more self-contradictory of the two doctrines.
[33] De Tocqueville, *op. cit.*, p. 149.
[34] *Ibid.*, p. 310.

entails, although Rousseau would go considerably beyond de Tocqueville in rejecting representative institutions altogether. Rousseau is quite unequivocal in his claims that excessive preoccupation with purely private interests while the public interest is represented means a renunciation of freedom and autonomy: ". . . the moment a people provides itself with represeentatives, it is no longer free: it no longer exists." [35] The privatization which gives rise to the desire for representation is the sign of a corrupt society:

> In a well-ordered city everyone flies to the assemblies: under a bad government no one wants to take a step to get there; because no one is interested in what happens there, because it is foreseen that the general will will not prevail, and finally because domestic cares absorb everything. . . . As soon as anyone says of the affairs of the State *What does it matter to me?* the state may be given up for lost.[36]

Privatization means the renunciation of self-mastery. Rousseau thus reveals the ultimate contradiction of a theory which associates liberty with privatization: "Is liberty maintained only with the support of slavery?" [37]

In light of Rousseau's comments on the effects of privatization and his implicit attack on the liberal theory of the state, it is illuminating to compare liberal conceptions of the public interest to Rousseau's concept of the general will, which is often regarded as a prime example of the abstraction and elevation of society over and against the individual. On the face of it, Rousseau seems to be constructing the kind of fictional community,

---

35 Jean-Jacques Rousseau, *Du Contrat social,* in *Œuvres Complètes,* III, 431 (Bk. III, chap. 15): ". . . à l'instant qu'un Peuple se donne des Réprésentans, il n'est plus libre; il n'est plus."
36 *Ibid.,* p. 429: "Dans un cité bien conduite chacun vole aux assemblées; sous un mauvais Gouvernement nul n'aime à faire un pas pour s'y rendre; parce que nul ne prend intérêt à ce qui s'y fait, qu'on prévoit que la volonté générale n'y dominera pas, et qu'enfin les soins domestiques absorbent tout. . . . Sitôt que que qu'un dit des affaires de l'Etat *que m'importe?* on doit compter que l'Etat est perdu."
37 *Ibid.,* p. 431: "Quoi! la liberté ne se maintient qu'à l'appui de la servitude?"

the "imaginary sovereignty" in which men are imaginary members, of which Marx is so critical; but it can be argued that he is, in fact, trying to avoid the objectification of society in the form of the state which is inherent in the philosophy of civil society. Although unlike Marx, Rousseau still speaks in terms of *political* society and political sovereignty, in his attempt to find a principle of politics compatible with true individual autonomy Rousseau seems to be seeking the reappropriation of society by the individual, the autonomy of the individual living in society, of which Marx writes. It can be argued that the concept of the general will is an expression of Rousseau's quest for precisely that reunification of public and private within individual men, that recovery by them of alien social power, which Marx describes.[38] And again like Marx, Rousseau recognizes that in or-

---

[38] Since Rousseau is still operating within the context of the *state,* and since the absorption of the private realm by the public coercive power of the state is regarded as an essential characteristic of totalitarianism, it must be emphasized that this absorption is not what Rousseu has in mind and that his "reunification" of public and private is not to be confused with eradication of any distinction between the two. The point here is simply that Rousseau is seeking a mode of association in which the individual is the bearer of his own social existence and that existence is not merely a fiction or an abstraction. As for the distinction between matters of "public" concern and matters of "private" concern, matters which are properly subject to the coercive power of the state and those which are not—a distinction which has proved so elusive in all doctrines which regard it as significant—this *is* recognized by Rousseau. (In fact, it is precisely his treatment of this question, with his distinctions between the "public person" and the "private persons" which compose it, or between the "rights of a man as citizen" and his rights as "man," which presents the difficulties we are about to discuss in our comparison of Rousseau and Marx.) And if Rousseau fails to deal with the distinction to our satisfaction, the same can be said of its most liberal expositors, not least of all, J. S. Mill in his famous opposition of "self-regarding" and "other-regarding" actions.

In a chapter of the *Social Contract* entitled, significantly, "The Limits of Sovereign Power," Rousseau writes: "It must be granted that each man gives up by the social contract only that part of his power, his goods, his liberty [the use of] which has a bearing on the community. . . .

". . . the Sovereign, for its part, cannot impose upon the subjects any bonds which are useless to the community." *Du Contrat social* in *Œuvres Complètes,* III, 373 (Bk. II, chap 4): ("On convient que tout ce que chacun aliéne par le pacte social de sa puissance, de ses biens, de sa liberté, c'est seulement la partie de tout cela dont l'usage emporte à la communauté. . . .

der to accomplish that recovery by the individual of his public being which alone permits individual autonomy, society must be reconstructed to heal the cleavages of civil society, cleavages that are simply taken for granted by the liberals who for that reason cannot conceive of autonomous men whose public beings are not represented by a power alien to them.

Such a comparison must, of course, be made with caution, since Marx so explicitly rejects a *political* solution like that apparently proposed by Rousseau. If, however, Rousseau is unavoidably bound by the limits of his epoch and cannot foresee the development of productive forces which Marx regards as an essential precondition to the genuine "reappropriation of social power"; if Rousseau's *solution* is therefore still too "political" for Marx and his language still too suggestive of the "liberalbourgeois" split between civil society and the state, his perception of the *problem* is so strikingly different from that of his contemporaries and so prophetic of Marx's own that the comparison seems worth making.

A consideration of Marx's attack on the Jacobin conception of politics and revolution may suffice to make this point. It is

---

". . . le Souverain de son coté ne peut charger les sujets d'aucune chaine inutile à la communauté.)

As vague as this may be, it is hardly more so than Locke's proposition that "the power of the Society, or the Legislative constituted by them, can never be suppos'd to extend further than the common good" *(Second Treatise* in *Two Treatises of Government, op. cit.,* p. 398, art. 131), or Mill's almost too facile formulation of the relation between the individual and the authority of society: "Each will receive its proper share if each has that which more particularly concerns it. To individuality should belong the part of life in which it is chiefly the individual that is interested; to society, the part which chiefly interests society. ("On Liberty" in *Essential Works of John Stuart Mill* [New York, Bantam Books, 1961], chap. IV, p. 322.

And if Rousseau makes us uneasy with his admission that the Sovereign is sole judge of what "concerns" society, are we any more comfortable with Locke's failure to tell us who is to determine the "common good," or Mill's failure to specify who is to be responsible for distinguishing between self- and other-regarding actions? Indeed, common sense and the very nature of political order would suggest that inevitably society—or rather its representative, the state—will judge, and that both Locke and Mill, no less than Rousseau, will grant the state the legal, if not the moral, right to do so.

more than ironic that Rousseau is so often regarded as the mentor of the Jacobins, when it is precisely to the degree that he seems to anticipate the possibility of a Jacobin solution that he also seems to foreshadow the Marxist critique.

One must, to begin with, distinguish between two aspects of Marx's "critique" of the French Revolution. There is, of course, his characterization of that event as simply a bourgeois revolution. This characterization can hardly be called an indictment, given Marx's view that historical circumstances and the development of productive relations as yet allowed nothing more. In this respect, the French Revolution was a praiseworthy, even a heroic, event, marking the destruction of the last vestiges of feudalism. On the other hand, it cannot be denied that Marx has little sympathy for the particular form taken by that bourgeois revolution, and that he ascribes its grave mistakes in large part to the faulty theoretical perspective of the revolutionary heroes, a misperception of the relationship between state and society and a narrow and excessively "political" conception of revolution. If historical circumstances precluded the occurrence of anything more progressive than a bourgeois revolution, the same circumstances did *not* render the Terror inevitable. In a very important sense, the Terror was made inevitable by the false theoretical principle upon which the Revolution was conducted. As Avineri points out,

> ... Jacobin terror is to Marx an attempt of the political state, emancipated and separated from civil society, to re-impose itself on civil society, to crush the private and particular interests realised in civil society. The Jacobin dictatorship attempts to overcome the antagonism between state and civil society by force, and the failure of such an attempt is immanent: the dichotomy between state and civil society cannot be overcome by the politization of civil society but only through a synthesis of particularism and universalism brought about by the recognition of the universality of the individual.[39]

The French Revolution in its Jacobin form, then, is in a sense

[39] Avineri, *op. cit.*, p. 189.

the liberal bourgeois state taken to extremes. Again, the state forcibly imposes itself upon civil society from without; and the false "universality" of society, the fictional community, is objectified and embodied in an alien power, the state, which inevitably becomes the instrument, not of the community, but of a *particular* will. But in this case, while the Jacobin revolution is still based on the fundamental contradictions inherent in civil society, at the same time it follows to its ultimate and necessarily violent conclusion the attempt of the bourgeois state to avoid the *consequences* of those contradictions by means of political order, legislation, and, above all, punishment. The failure to recognize the futility of such an effort and its inevitably bloody culmination is a consequence of "political" thinking—the kind of thinking that, as Marx argues, fails to

> ... seek the basis of *social* evils and to grasp the *general* explanation of them in the *principle of the State,* itself, that is, in the *structure of society,* of which the State is the active, conscious, and official expression. *Political* thought is really *political* thought in the sense that the thinking takes place within the framework of politics. The clearer and more vigorous political thought is, the *less* it is able to grasp the nature of social evils. The *classical* period of political thought is the *French Revolution.*[40]

It would perhaps be too much to argue that in seeking a solution to social evils Rousseau entirely escapes the narrow "bourgeois" perspective of the Jacobins, since his vision, no less than theirs, must be limited by the stage that relations of production have attained in his era. Nevertheless, it can certainly be said that his theoretical approach, his perception of the social problem, and his objectives are qualitatively different from those of the Jacobins and come much closer to Marx's. To begin with, if one regards Rousseau's major works as a unity, as he clearly

---

40 Marx, "Kritische Randglossen zu dem Artikel: Der König von Preussen und die Sozial-reform, Von einem Preussen," *Vorwärts,* 7 August 1844, quoted in T. B. Bottomore and Maximilien Rubel, *Karl Marx: Selected Writings in Sociology and Social Philosophy* (Harmondsworth: Penguin Books, 1963), pp. 223–224.

did himself (notably the "Discourse on the Origin of Inequality," *Emile*, and *The Social Contract*); if, for example, one takes seriously his claim that everything in *The Social Contract* is already in the "Discourse on the Origin of Inequality," it becomes clear that Rousseau, unlike the Jacobins, is *not* a "political" thinker in Marx's sense. For Rousseau, as for Marx, the state is the "active and conscious expression" of the social structure, the social structure is the "principle" of the state. The civil order arose out of the contradictions inherent in the development of private property and the consequent class antagonisms; the state has ever since its inception always and *necessarily* been the instrument of a ruling class, the instrument of an economically superior class; and as long as the structure of society remains the same, the contradictions in civil society will persist and the state will continue to exist as an oppressive alien power:

> In the civil state there is a chimerical and vain equality of right, because the means which are designed to maintain it themselves destroy it, and because the public power joins the stronger to oppress the weak and destroys the kind of equilibrium which nature has established between them. [Rousseau's note: The universal spirit of the laws of every country always favors the strong against the weak, and him who has against him who has not; this defect is inevitable, and there is no exception.] From this first contradiction are derived all the other contradictions between the real and the apparent that can be observed in the civil order. The multitude will always be sacrificed to a small number, and public interest to particular interest. The specious words, justice and subordination, will always serve as the instruments of violence and the arms of iniquity: From which it follows that the higher classes which pretend to be useful to others are useful only to themselves at the expense of others. . . .[41]

41 Rousseau, *Emile*, in *Œuvres Complètes*, IV, 524 (Book IV: "Il y a dans l'état civil une égalité de droit chimerique et vaine, parce que les moyens destinés à la maintenir servent eux-mêmes à la détruire; et que la force publique ajouté au plus fort pour opprimer le foible, rompt l'espèce d'équilibre que la Nature avoit mis entr'eux. [*Note*: L'esprit universel des Loix de tous les pays est de favoriser toujours le fort contre le foible, et celui qui a, contre celui qui n'a rien; cet inconvénient est inévitable, et il est sans exception.] De cette première contradiction découlent toutes celles qu'on remarque dans l'ordre civil, entre l'apparence et la réalité. Toujours la mul-

Here, Rousseau seems to go so far as to reject a political solution altogether. It is significant that he so utterly rejects politics when he is giving an account of the "corrupt" society—in the "Discourses" on the arts and sciences and on inequality or in the relevant parts of *Emile*—that instead of calling for political reform, he dismisses the civil order as inevitably evil. He is anti-political in his account of such a society precisely because, since the state is the expression of the social structure, it is impossible to conceive and absurd to speak of *any* "good" political order in the context of a fundamentally corrupt society. Although, like Marx, Rousseau prefers certain ages in the history of man to others and has praise for certain social orders—particularly in classical antiquity—it is clear that on the whole he concludes that, just as there has never been a social order not based on gross class divisions since the development of property and class antagonisms made the state necessary, there has never been a truly just political order. The political order became necessary because of property and class relations and has ever since been an expression of these relations. Politics can be embraced or rejected only to the extent that the underlying social relations are regarded as good or evil. Thus, it is possible to embrace politics only in a radically transmuted form, as the expression of a radically transformed society such as the world has probably not yet known.

Seen from this perspective, the so-called contradictions between the political concerns of *The Social Contract,* on the one hand, and the attacks on the civil order of the first two "Discourses," on the other, disappear. It is precisely *because* he regards the state as the expression of the social structure that Rousseau, the political theorist of *The Social Contract,* can at the same time be the notoriously anti-political thinker of the "Dis-

titude sera sacrifiée au petit nombre, et l'intérêt public à l'intérêt particulier. Toujours ces noms spécieux de justice et de subordination serviront d'instrumens à la violence et d'armes à l'iniquité: d'où il suit que les ordres distingués qui se prétendent utiles aux autres, ne sont, en effet, utiles qu'à eux-mêmes au dépens des autres. . . ."

courses" and *Emile*. *The Social Contract* assumes as a prior condition the transformation of human relations that the "Discourses" and *Emile* outline as necessary. The point is that only the existence of certain kinds of *social* relations makes even the desired *political* relations possible; individuals existing in the antagonistic relations of civil society cannot become the source of the general will, and yet the general will cannot, by definition, originate in any *other* source than the whole community of associated individuals. In short, the general will cannot be expressed at all until the fundamental nature of social relations changes. Thus, for example, when, in his remarkably prophetic warnings against the passive subjection of individuals in society to an alien power and the ultimate embodiment of that alien power in the particular will of a Robespierre, Rousseau writes:

> If then the people promises simply to obey, it dissolves itself by that act, it loses that which makes it a people; the moment there is a master, there is no longer a Sovereign, and from then on the body politic is destroyed.[42]

or:

> . . . according to the fundamental compact, only the general will can bind individuals, and one can never be sure that a particular will conforms to the general will. . . .

the significance of these statements goes beyond their immediate political meaning, beyond their rejection of the "enlightened" dictatorship of a Robespierre or their a priori denial of any man's claim to represent the general will. The point is that the existence of a "master," on the one hand, or a genuine "Sov-

---

[42] Rousseau, *Du Contrat social*, III, 369. Book II, chap. 1: "Si donc le peuple promet simplement d'obéir, il se dissout par cet acte, il perd sa qualité de peuple; à l'instant qu'il y a un maître il n'y a plus de Souverain, et dès lors le corps politique est détruit."

[43] *Ibid.*, p. 383 (chap. 7): ". . . le peuple même ne peut, quand il le voudroit, se dépouiller de ce droit incommunicable; parce que selon le pacte fondamental il n'y a que la volonté générale qui oblige les particuliers, et qu'on ne peut jamais s'assurer qu'une volonté particulière est conforme à la volonté générale. . . ."

ereign," on the other, is not a matter of chance or even simply of *will*, but rather to a significant extent a function of the underlying social, and especially class, relations; and the possibility of a "Sovereign," the community of individuals who in free association with each other can be the only source of the general will, depends upon a really fundamental change in those relations from those that have prevailed in all hitherto existing societies, which have inevitably been characterized by "masters," a ruling class. It can perhaps be said that in this respect Rousseau is seeking the *reabsorption* of the state by society, and precisely that "synthesis of pacticularism and universalism," that "recognition of the universality of the individual," to which Avineri referred in writing of Marx. In the final analysis, then, *The Social Contract* is perhaps as anti-political as are the other works, in the sense that the principle of "politics" embodied in the "Sovereign" involves a kind of "withering away of the state" in the Marxist sense—the state as a coercive instrument of a ruling class—and the replacement of the state by "politics" in a very different sense, so different that it may come closer to Marx's "self-activity of associated individuals" than it does to "politics" as it is commonly understood.

It must be emphasized, then, that for Rousseau, as for Marx, the primary objective is the transformation of human relations. Thus, while the Jacobins strive forcibly to impose a new political order upon the contradictions of civil society, Rousseau wants to go to the very heart of the contradictions, to surpass civil society and its concomitant state, to make a genuinely new form of association possible. Moreover, if Rousseau is unable to give a satisfactory account of how such a fundamental *social* change is to come about, it is at least clear—and this is profoundly significant—that for him, the underlying material conditions would not be as incidental to social change as they are for the Jacobins. Rousseau's conception of the origin and evolution of society as depicted in the "Discourse on the Origin of Inequality" is, again, strikingly prophetic of Marx in its emphasis on property, on developments in the "means of production"—e.g. "corn" and "iron" symbolizing agriculture and metallurgy—as the mainspring of social change, and on the division of labor, even down to the details of the successive social divisions of labor.[44]

To return, then, to Rousseau's concept of the general will, it cannot be emphasized enough that the general will is *not* an abstraction distinct from the wills of individuals living in society. Quite the contrary, it is the public expression of individual men whose private and public wills no longer conflict to such an extent that their "public will" must be expressed by an alien power, because they no longer exist in a society the very essence of which is antagonism. Above all, as we have seen the general will cannot be represented, either, as those like Robespierre would have it, by a single man or group, or even, as the liberals propose, by a representative body of "extraordinary" men.[45] Nor is the general will some kind of "collective consciousness," but rather, if anything, the expression of an individual consciousness capable, as it were, of universalizing itself, perhaps an individual consciousness capable of *compassion*. But maybe even this metaphor makes the concept of the general will appear to be more mystical or romantic than it is. Very

44 See, for example, Engels' account of social evolution in *The Origin of the Family, Private Property, and the State,* where Engels claims to be fulfilling the bequest of Marx by presenting the ideas of the American anthropologist L. H. Morgan as support for Marx's own conclusions about human history. Although this account of social history is attributed to Morgan, the similarities to Rousseau's account are striking.

45 It is also interesting to compare Rousseau's remarks on the size of the ideal commonwealth with those of Madison: "If I had been able to choose the place of my birth, I should have chosen a society which had a size commensurate with the limits of human faculties, that is, with the possibility of being well governed, and in which everyone being equal to his occupation, no one should be forced to commit to others the functions with which he was charged." "Discours sur l'origine de l'inégalité," in *Œuvres Complétes,* III, 111–112: "Si j'avois eu à choisir le lieu de ma naissance, j'aurois choisi une société d'une grandeur bornée par l'étendue des facultés humaines, c'est à dire par la possibilité d'être bien gouvernée, et ou chacun suffisant à son emploi, nul n'eût contraint de commetre à d'autres les fonctions dont il étoit chargé. . . ."

simply, the general will can be seen as a principle of *procedure*, almost a rule of thumb according to which the citizens is to ask himself when deliberating on a matter of public concern, "Is this for the common good?" rather than "Is this in the interests of a particular man or group?" That it is the posing of the question, with the added condition that it be posed to each member of the community of citizens, and not the content of the answer that is the essence of Rousseau's idea of the general will is suggested by the following observation: "Thus the rule of public order in assemblies is not so much to maintain the general will there, as to ensure that it [the general will in each man] always be consulted and that it always respond." [46] Nevertheless, if the concept of the general will is a principle of political procedure, it is one that has certain social preconditions Without that reconstruction of society that will heal the basic cleavages and lessen the antagonism between the individual's public and private beings, the effective implementation of the procedure is impossible. In this sense, the general will represents not only the procedural rule, but also a shorthand expression of the social conditions necessary for its implementation. In short, it can perhaps be said that the concept of the general will expresses the principle that ordinary individuals in Rousseau's society can to a significant extent be expected to act as Locke, Madison, and Mill expect their enlightened, prudent, and virtuous representatives to act, *without* violating their individual wills. The concept of the general will means, in effect, that all men are their own representatives, capable of expressing "opinions" as well as "interests," to use Hannah Arendt's distinction.[47] In short, the general will is the will of individuals who have "taken back into [themselves] the abstract citizen . . . so that social force is no

---

[46] Rousseau, *Du Contrat social*, p. 438 (Bk. IV, chap. I): "Ainsi la loi de l'ordre publique dans les assemblées n'est pas tant d'y maintenir la volonté générale, que de faire qu'elle soit toujours interrogée et qu'elle réponde toujours."

[47] Hannah Arendt, *On Revolution*, chap. 6. Miss Arendt would not, of course, approve of this application of her ideas to Rousseau—especially since she tends to treat Rousseau as if he were Robespierre. This is not the

longer separated from [them] as political power" [48] embodied
in an alien state.

The significant point here is that by making the individual
the source of the general will, Rousseau is emphasizing the active participation of the individual and, above all, the principle
that the individual is the source of universality. Objectivity and
universality, as expressed in the general will or the public interest, instead of having a separate and alien existence distinct
from the "private" realm of the individual or subject, now become functions of subjectivity. In a sense, then, Rousseau's political doctrine can be understood as an anticipation, in moral
rather than epistemological theory, of the Kantian reunification
of subject and object and the principle that the subject is itself

---

place to discuss specifically her misrepresentations of Rousseau. The suggestion here is simply that, in a certain sense, her distinction between interest
and opinion may perhaps be usefully applied to Rousseau's distinction
between particular and general will as it is understood here. At least, the
general will is very much a "political" phenomenon—not an abstraction, not
a "will" imposed from above, not even the kind of almost mystical spiritual
unison which Miss Arendt seems to attribute to Rousseau's society, but
rather a phenomenon which arises only out of active participation in the
public space by men of independent mind. It should perhaps be noted, for
example, that contrary to Miss Arendt's suggestion—cf. *ibid.*, p. 244—Rousseau's objection to "partial" associations—whatever else can be said against
it—at least does not spring from a fear that they will endanger unanimity,
but, on the contrary, from the conviction that they endanger independent
thought. (See *Du Contrat social*, Bk. II, chap. 3.) In this respect, modern
studies of groups would tend to confirm some of Rousseau's fears, and it is
perhaps significant that the social scientists referred to earlier, who regard
political apathy as "functional," often seem to regard the existence of inter-
mediate groups as a means of rendering political impotence palatable to the
masses and, hence, as a "functional equivalent," as it were, for political
apathy.

After my manuscript went to the printer, I had occasion to look more
deeply into the question of Rousseau's attitude to "partial societies." I
now think that in my reference to it in this note, I have conceded too
much to Hannah Arendt's interpretation, and to all the arguments that
make so much of Rousseau's supposed objection to voluntary associations.
It is clear to me now that, not only are Rousseau's objections not what
Arendt claims they are but, in fact, he has no objections to voluntary
associations in the sense intended—indeed, he welcomes them. A careful
consideration of his works and his correspondence should make it clear
that the "partial societies" to which he objects are the great and powerful,

the source of objectivity and universality.[49] Seen in this light, an interpretation of Rousseau can act as a further gloss on Marx's statements concerning civil society and human society and their respective relationships to certain epistemological theories.

---

above all intolerant, "parties," notably the "devout" party, the priests and nobles who, according to Rousseau, use religious superstition to suppress the people; and their rivals, the "party of the philosophes," who equally intolerantly attack religion for their own questionable purposes. These are "partial societies'" precisely in the sense that they rend society apart in their intolerant contentions and are a primary cause of civil strife and intolerance. In this respect, Rousseau is no different from, say, John Locke. Locke is never accused of attacking voluntary associations (in fact, he can be credited with at least an implicit pluralistic theory of politics based on voluntary associations), and yet he is as violent as Rousseau in his attacks on powerful, intolerant, and contentious "parties," largely religious groups, which "blind men's understanding" and foment civil discord.

As for voluntary associations in the usual sense—clubs, for example—one need only consider Rousseau's eulogy of the *"cercles"* of Geneva in his "Letter to d'Alembert," and his staunch defense of those clubs and their social and political functions (notably in the protection of liberty), when he was attacked by some fellow Genevans for his advocacy of their clubs, which the magistrates of Geneva were to denounce a few years later as hotbeds of opposition to the Petit Conseil. (Incidentally, Rousseau's advocacy of clubs is more explicit than anything Locke seems ever to have written in favor of voluntary associations.) See, for example, Rousseau's letter to Théodore Tronchin of November 26, 1758 (in the R. A. Leigh edition of the correspondence, no. 743, V, 241–242; or Dufour-Plan edition, no. 581), which is devoted entirely to this question and in which, among other things, Rousseau distinguishes the Republic of Geneva, with its clubs, from monarchies, "where all subjects must remain isolated and must have nothing in common but obedience."

48 See above, p. 151, n. 22, for citation.

49 Of course, Kant himself gives the epistemological principle an immediate "practical" meaning in his own moral doctrine—for example, in his categorical imperative, which involves a kind of universifiable subjectivity.

Conclusion

Having raised some of the questions about politics and society, liberty and community, implicit in certain epistemological problems, one is, of course, inclined to ask to what extent these questions are still issues in contemporary thought. It is worth noting, therefore, that the controversy over the nature of mind that has been discussed in this essay seems now to have been transposed from philosophy to the social sciences and, in a sense, intellectual history is repeating itself on another plane. Again, a theory of the creative mind—this time proposed by modern social scientists like the linguistic theoriest Noam Chomsky and the psychologist Jean Piaget—is challenging the passive empiricism that prevails in so much of the behavioral sciences. And like the earlier debate on the nature of the human mind, this one is reflected in conceptions of politics and the nature of human community and freedom. It may, then, be appropriate to conclude this essay with a brief summary of the more universal moral and political questions raised by what, superficially, is simply an epistemological problem, and to consider the meaning of these questions for modern political science in particular.

Needless to say, the controversy over the nature of mind has a great deal to do with the question of man's place in the natural order. Is the human mind to be regarded simply as a responsive cog in the mechanism of nature, or is it a creative, determinative force? Moreover, our conceptions of the "political" will ultimately depend on where we place man in the universal machine. For the classical Greeks, for example, the realm of the political was the realm of freedom, of the truly human, in which man raised himself above the rest of the natural order, above his determined, simply animal life, above the realm of pure necessity.

Political life was the realm of transcendence, the life of conscious, purposeful action, in which man as a rational being in a sense participated in the divine as a creator and, at least in part, a master of his fate, instead of simply a creature blindly responding to natural, biological necessity. Perhaps one might say, to return to our earlier language, that the political realm was precisely that realm in which man was the subject, not simply the object, of history. The science of politics, then, since it was concerned with purposeful *action,* was necessarily a moral science, rather than, as it were, a pure natural science dealing simply with "behavior."

It is perhaps significant that, with the rise of the "modern" natural sciences, the meaning of politics changed profoundly. Whether the relationship between developments in the natural sciences and changes in the conception of politics is historical, logical, or simply coincidental, there is at least a heuristic value in speaking of the relationship as if it were not purely accidental. In any case, in the wake of striking achievements in the physical sciences, culminating in Newton's work, there developed a strong compulsion, already in the seventeenth century and particularly in the eighteenth, to establish social and political sciences modeled on the physical sciences and possessing the same kind of precision and exactitude. It is perhaps no coincidence that a strong faith in an exact social science was so often associated, from Hobbes to J. S. Mill, with advocacy of doctrines central to the growth of liberalism. It can be argued that some of the unique characteristics of liberalism—its conception of man, society, and politics—were eminently suited to this inclination toward a Newtonian science of society and politics.

In order to conceive of a social science modeled on the natural sciences, it was necessary to transfer, so to speak, the realm of nature to the social world, to convert social forces into natural forces. This development was more than a little ironic. On the one hand, the notion of man's transcendence of the predictably regular natural order was preserved in the potentially dangerous doctrine of man's domination of nature, which had played such an important part in the rise of natural science and which continued to flourish in the theory and practice of capitalism. On the other hand, the new social science *denied* this transcendence in the very realm that is most distinctively human, the realm of society, transforming the social order into a "natural" phenomenon over which men did not exercise mastery, since they were themselves the predictable basic elements, the "atoms," as it were, which constituted it.[1] Clearly, a social system that is most amenable to this kind of analysis is one in which men are treated as objects, as passive functions of regular, independently existing objective forces. It has been suggested throughout this essay that precisely such a conception of society is embodied in liberalism, and possibly even in the historical reality it reflects.

It will perhaps be recalled that a suggestion as to the nature of this connection between liberalism and a particular kind of social science appears in Marx. Such a suggestion is certainly implicit, for example, in the formula proposed in the *Theses on Feuerbach,* in which Marx speaks of the tendency of materialism to conceive of the world "only in the form of *objects of observations"* rather than as "practical activity," "subjectively," and associates this tendency with a particular conception of society and politics, a conception expressed in the concept of "civil society."[2] It has been argued in this essay that the philosophers of civil society tend to regard man as an *object,* as a function of independent objective forces, and to regard the *good* society as one in which these forces are allowed to operate more or less freely and man is permitted to enjoy freely his objective role in

---

1 By contrast, Marx, who already began to deplore the destructive aspect of the doctrine of the domination of nature, demanded a social order of which man *is* the master, at least in part in order to establish a less destructive and more harmonious relationship with nature.

2 Karl Marx, *Theses on Feuerbach,* in Karl Marx, *Selected Writings in Sociology and Social Philosophy,* ed. T. B. Bottomore and M. Rubel (Harmondsworth: Penguin Books, 1963), Thesis I, p. 82.

that operation. If civil society is so conceived, then clearly it becomes a particularly suitable object for "scientific" observation. In other words, if society operates like a natural mechanism, and man as a unit of that mechanism is to be regarded as an object of observation like any other natural phenomenon, it is convenient that, like a natural phenomenon, he *behaves* rather than *acts*, that he responds predictably to the regular operations of natural mechanisms. Insofar as man in his social life is regarded as an appropriate object for exact scientific observation—that is, as simply a part of the "natural" order—there is a tendency to minimize his "subjectivity," his creative self-activity, his role as a conscious, purposeful actor. In such a case, the meaning of human freedom in general, and of politics in particular, must, of course, be adjusted accordingly.

It is one of the most striking accomplishments of liberalism that it seems to have found a concept of social freedom that can reconcile a faith in the orderly, predictable, mechanistically determined operation of society—comparable to the operation of physical forces—with a commitment to individual liberty. In its definition of freedom, liberalism, ideally, frees the individual to a great extent from human authority by subjecting him to the impersonal authority of mechanistic social forces. In so doing, it has in a sense satisfied both the demands of individual liberty and those of scientific order and predictability. Politics correspondingly becomes simply a regulatory force designed to maintain the existing order, perhaps a feedback mechanism that promotes homeostasis, inherent in and subordinate to the new "natural" order of society, rather than transcending or purposefully changing that order. To put it another way, politics has been relegated to the realm which for the Greeks was the realm of biological necessity, of day-to-day animal existence, "household management," *oikonomia*.

It can be argued that Marx's purpose was precisely to elaborate a conception of freedom, in practical social and political terms, that would preserve the liberal concern for individual liberty while at the same time not denying to man his mastery of history and social forces, a conception of freedom that in a sense would remove human social life from the purely natural order. If this is the case, however, something must, of course, be said about Marx's own convictions concerning the possibility of an exact social science. In the past it has been so common to emphasize Marx's pretensions as a scientist that certain essential premises of his doctrine have often been overlooked. We have already referred to certain misconceptions regarding Marx's materialism and determinism. Needless to say, it is precisely to the extent that Marx is regarded as a believer in a simplistic science of society and in the precise predictability of human behavior that he must also be regarded as a crude determinist. On the other hand, it is far too simple to dismiss altogether Marx's scientific claims, as certain "Marxist humanists" may seem to do. The problem, of course, is to reconcile Marx's social science with his conception of man and his faith in the efficacy of purposeful human action. That faith in action—creative *revolutionary* action —necessarily implies a doubt about the ultimate possibility of a social science in the narrow sense, insofar as revolutionary action presupposes that man can become the subject of history, that he can transcend the determined, regular order of "nature." Nor was Marx himself unconscious of this paradox. Indeed, it can be said that he deliberately formulated a social science that has this paradox as its very essence. To begin with, while he certainly believed in the possibility of scientifically discovering the laws of all "hitherto existing" societies, his criticism of those societies, paticularly of capitalist systems, was in a sense precisely that they made an exact science of history and society all too possible by forcing men to be the passive playthings of historical "laws." This situation represented for Marx simply the period of prehistory. The stage of *human* history which he sought to initiate would begin only when men ceased to be cogs in the machine and became self-active, creative subjects, that is, highly unsatisfactory objects for exact scientific observation and prediction.

An understanding of the thitherto operative social and historical laws was a necessary precondition to the establishment of human history, in which those laws would no longer be independently operative. In this sense, then, the purpose of Marx's social science was, as it were, to make an "exact" or positivistic social science impossible.

Marx's criticism of early materialism, therefore, was not simply that it had failed to discover the true laws of history, but also that its conception of man failed to take into account the possibility of his transcendence of those laws. Such a conception of man was not only scientifically inaccurate in that it tended to oversimplify the nature of man, but morally wrong, insofar as it encouraged the treatment of men as *things*—and, perhaps, insofar as its proponents could not help but be attracted to "civil society," in theory and practice, with its externalization of man, its reduction of man to a manifestation of interest, class, the division of labor, the market, and so on. Moreover, the implicit denial of man's capacity to act, to initiate revolutionary change, was a tacit argument for the perpetuation of existing evils.

The significance of Marx's social science is further revealed by a comparison with certain more recent developments in the "science" of society. In a very important sense, the prevailing trends in modern, especially American, social science, particularly in the last two or three decades, has represented a return to early pre-Marxist materialism-empiricism; and to the extent that it adheres to the premises of those earlier doctrines, it tends to secrete similar social and political values. In its conception of man, modern social science has gone a good deal further than its materialist predecessors in reducing man to an externalized function of objective forces, in reducing "action" to "behavior." This further reduction of man has accompanied the demand for an even more simplistic science of society. Any other conception of man would tend to complicate matters for the social scientist with his faith in precise prediction, quantification, and measurement. Associated with these conceptions of man and society are certain implicit ideological assumptions concerning the meaning of freedom, action, politics, and the good society.

At first glance, there would seem to be little difference between Marx's notion of a social science as preparation for "human history," and the contemporary social scientist's claim that he wants to *know* in order to be able to *control*. If, however, such a claim is meant to reflect man's capacity to transcend seemingly autonomous social forces, it is a deceptive claim when associated with a social science that fails to incorporate into its very core—indeed, seems to deny—a recognition of that capacity and a rejection of the necessary autonomy of social forces. The point is that, for Marx, the conception of man as the subject of his history—and not simply the passive object—is not extraneous to his social science, even when it is examing man as object; it is a dimension that is always an integral part of his science, always part of the data, as it were. Thus, for example, for Marx it becomes the task of the social scientist not only to discover social and historical laws, but to explain why they exist at all, given man's creative, autonomous nature; not simply to document the autonomy of social forces, but to explain why they appear autonomous; and perhaps even to regard the simple predictability of social forces as a human failure to be overcome, rather than a technical advance to be achieved. In other words, man as a function of objective and independently existing historical forces must always be examined in terms of man as the *creator* of history.[3]

The case with modern social science is, of course, rather different, and this is true not only of explicitly quantitative "behavioral" political science, which must reduce human life to the most simplistically quantifiable externalized factors of behavior, but perhaps even more significantly of other approaches—such as "structural-functional" or "systems" theories, etc.—which do not necessarily concern themselves directly with quantification. One of the most striking features of contemporary political sci-

[3] In this sense, Marx's humanism and his social science need not be seen as mutually contradictory. His social science *embodies* his humanism.

ence is the extent to which it depends on conceiving of man solely as a reflexive function of his objective position in an independently operating social structure. Men, who are in essence *participants* in a social system, are possessors of *roles*—or "functionally defined positions" in a social system. Roles are institutionalized forms of behavior, and men, as the "occupants" of several roles, are essentially little more than points at which several objective and independently existing roles intersect. Such an approach to the science of society is certainly very different from one in which social processes are discussed, not only as a working-out of causal relations among abstract and independently existing "roles" and "functions," but as the results of human *actions* and *ends* which may simply have been, to quote Sartre, "neutralized at the heart of the historical process of totalization"[4]—a process of neutralization that can potentially be overcome, in its turn, by human action.

In view of their mode of conceptualization, it is not difficult to understand why so many modern political scientists seem to have such a predilection for the liberal values of "civil society," why even their "empirical definitions" of politics are impregnated with these values.[5] A society true to the liberal model of a good society as a smoothly operating mechanism consisting of a network of externalized, perhaps institutionalized, social interactions (an image to which the concept of the market is so eminently suited), in which man's freedom consists in the relatively unobstructed enjoyment of his role, would clearly be the modern social scientist's dream. Thus, the old liberal concept of *interest,* with the suggestion that society is a web of interacting interests

[4] Jean-Paul Sartre, *Search for a Method,* trans. Hazel Barnes (New York: Vintage Books, 1968), p. 158.
[5] It must be emphasized that the argument here is not simply that many political scientists also happen to have a commitment to the values of liberalism which is sometimes revealed in their work. Instead, the suggestion is that the values of liberalism are contained in the very perceptual apparatus through which these men interpret the social world, so that these values appear unconsciously in their conceptual frameworks and in the ostensibly formal, so-called empirical, definitions with which they begin.

and politics a function of interest, serves the purposes of modern political science very well, and, in one form or another, plays a central role in most "empirical" definitions of politics. Significantly, these definitions of politics and society in terms of interest are meant to be universal and are not confined by political scientists to societies clearly reflecting the principle of "civil society," the social and economic context from which these concepts were originally drawn. Presumably, in the interest of science, all societies ought to conform to the liberal democratic model.

Another feature of the "new" political science which may be revealing is the conception of rationality that seems to prevail. This conception is particularly well illustrated in conflict theories, "game theory," and often in voting-behavior studies. Perhaps the most significant thing that can be said about it is that it is clearly based on the assumption that rational behavior is the most predictable behavior. While various political scientists may differ as to their faith in the degree of "rationality" that may actually be expected from men in the real world, there appears to be agreement that the ideal object for scientific observation and prediction is the rational man. On the face of it, this may seem to be a perfectly commonplace, perhaps even self-evident, assumption. Nevertheless, if one examines other conceptions of rationality, perhaps even those reflected in common usage, it must be conceded that the assumption is far from self-evident, that, in fact, perhaps the most common conceptions of rationality would suggest the contrary. Animal behavior, for example, is said to be nonrational, possibly for the very reason that it is more easily predictable than human behavior. The predictability of animal behavior lies in the narrow range of choices—if one can speak here of choice—available to a creature whose behavior is determined by the regular operation of its biological instinctual apparatus, uncomplicated by consciousness. Even *ir*rational human behavior—such as compulsive or psychotic behavior—may be more predictable than "rational" behavior precisely because the actions of an irrational man are beyond the control of his choice or reason and impelled by the inexorable "laws" of his compulsion or psychosis. It is surely a characteristic of human reason as it is generally conceived that it widens the options available to its possessor, making his behavior more flexible, more subtly changeable, and hence, presumably, less predictable. Nor, according to this notion, can human rationality be said to consist solely in a more complex capacity for means-end calculation, since the difference between what we call nonrational animals and rational men is precisely that, while animal "goals" are built into the instinctual apparatus, reason complicates matters by providing alternative goals. In a sense, then, man is said to be rational precisely insofar as he seems creatively to transcend the predictable natural order.

The argument that equates rational behavior with the most predictable behavior tends to equate human rationality with the *functionality* of a machine. In others words, the most "rational" phenomenon would be a well-oiled, efficient machine with preprogrammed, inflexible goals. This kind of conception of rationality is already suggested by the simplistic psychology of empiricism-liberalism, beginning with Hobbes and culminating in the felicific calculus of Bentham, the archetypal exponent of an exact, even quantitative, science of society. Such a psychology again tends to minimize the significance of conscious, purposeful, creative action and to replace it with reflexive behavior. This tendency is reflected in a particular conception of politics that is not comfortable with the idea of political action, of purposeful social change, nor the conception of politics as a means of mastering the "natural" order of history—or anything more than a regulatory, "homeostatic" mechanism subordinate to the existing social order. Still less can such a view conceive, for example, of the possibility envisaged by Marx that politics, in the form of the state as we know it, will ultimately give way to social action generated by self-active individuals. Instead, politics must remain a function of the "natural" order, which in the social realm means a function of "civil society" and the interaction of "interests."

All these views of man as the passive function of external forces may again be related to a particular conception of community, a conception which, it is true, may be simply a rather exaggerated and universalized reflection of the particular social reality from which it springs. It may be worth suggesting that the atomistic pluralism so popular in contemporary political science admirably reflects the situation described by Marx, in which the disunity among men and the atomization of social action gives history, as an aggregate of individual, antagonistic acts, a force and a meaning independent of human will, which, to quote Sartre again, "appears to men as a foreign force exactly insofar as they do not recognize the meaning of their enterprise . . . in the total, objective result." It may also not be idle to argue that the possibility of factoring out the individual wills of men, implicit in this situation, is the very condition that makes *statistics* and "aggregate data" such meaningful tools for the social scientist. Thus, the atomization of society seems again to be the condition for man's subjection to "autonomous" social laws. In fact, it can be argued that the most essential statistical procedures on which much of contemporary social science depends are possible *only* on the basis of a particular conception of community.[6] Apparently, the very mathematical possibility of these procedures rests on the implicit assumption that men are bound together, not by interpersonal relations, but by a network of independently existing social forces which act upon each of them in isolation. For example, if two voters "exhibit" the same voting "behavior," it would seem to be *not* because they communicate with each other, but because each one independently of the other has been subject to similar social forces or "variables."

In any case, in one form or another, the debate between "empirict-materialists" and advocates of the "creative

---

[6] I owe this suggestion to Professor E. J. H. Weissman of the Department of Political Science, York University, Toronto. Professor Weissman develops the argument extensively in an examination of the explicit and implicit assumptions underlying statistical methods in the social sciences, in an unpublished manuscript entitled *If Men Were Plants.*

mind," continues. In recent years, the challenge to empiricist-materialism in its modern incarnation, which has more or less held the field in much of social science, has become especially pressing as new theories of the creative mind—such as those of Piaget or Chomsky—have been elaborated. As before, it is perhaps not too much to say that the significance of this challenge may be as much moral or even political as it is scientific. At least, to view the controversy from this perspective, far from complicating the issue, may render the arguments more intelligible. Again, just as it is often difficult to grasp in any concrete terms the meaning of traditional epistemological disputes, except in light of the non-epistemological implications that may be drawn from them, much the same is true of many "scientific" controversies among social scientists. In the last analysis, does it really make sense, for example, to speak of *empirically* distinguishing between spontaneity and response, activity or passivity, as the essential principle of human behavior? Can the data really speak for themselves to that extent? On the one hand, behavioral psychology has shown us how easy it is to conjure away all apparent expressions of human creativity and agency simply by interpreting them a priori as "responses"—to perhaps unknown, but "in principle" knowable, stimuli. On the other hand, I venture to say that the "evidence" of self-experience will always obstinately challenge this interpretation and continue to force on us a belief in man's fundamental creativity, even to the extent of regarding ourselves as either "sick" or grossly misused when we feel a loss of agency; and that there will always be theorists who choose to accept this "evidence" supplied by their own self-experience. But if the problem finally eludes us at this level and we must always reach a point where the distinction between "action" and "behavior" becomes impossible to make "scientifically," it is not quite so difficult to distinguish between world views that emphasize one or the other aspect of man. If, then, we understand the controversy as in some sense representing a choice between different designs for man's life in society, the debate may not seem so ultimately fruitless.

Index